LUPITA MAÑANA

with
Connections

D0171182

LUPITA MAÑANA

By Patricia Beatty

with Connections

HOLT, RINEHART AND WINSTON
Harcourt Brace & Company

Austin • New York • Orlando • Atlanta • San Francisco
Boston • Dallas • Toronto • London

For permission to reprint copyrighted material, grateful acknowledgment is made to the following sources:

Morrow Junior Books and Beech Tree Paperbacks, divisions of William Morrow & Company, Inc.: *Lupita Mañana* by Patricia Beatty. Copyright © 1981 by Patricia Beatty.

Rose Del Castillo Guilbault: "Field Work" by Rose Del Castillo Guilbault from *The San Francisco Chronicle*, March 18, 1990. Copyright © 1990 by Rose Del Castillo Guilbault. *Naomi Shihab Nye:* "West Side" from *Hugging the Jukebox* by Naomi Shihab Nye. Copyright © 1982 by Naomi Shihab Nye. *University of Notre Dame Press:* From *Barrio Boy* by Ernesto Galarza. Copyright © 1971 by University of Notre Dame Press. *Viking Penguin, a division of Penguin Putnam Inc.:* "Helen Cohen, Poland," "Vartan Hartunian, Turkey (Armenian)," "Lazarus Salamon, Hungary," and "About Ellis Island and the Oral History Project" from *I Was Dreaming to Come to America* by Veronica Lawlor. Copyright © 1995 by Veronica Lawlor. *Charlie H. Wingfield, Jr.:* Excerpt (retitled "My Hands Are Like a History Book") by Charlie H. Wingfield from *The Black Americans, A History in Their Own Words: 1619–1983*, edited by Milton Meltzer. Copyright © 1962 by Charlie H. Wingfield.

Sources Cited: From *My Life* by Golda Meir. Published by Putnam Publishing Group, New York, 1975.

Cover illustration by Diane Bennett/Daniele Collignon Represents

BY PATRICIA BEATTY

Be Ever Hopeful, Hannalee

Behave Yourself, Bethany Brant

Charley Skedaddle

The Coach That Never Came

Eben Tyne, Powdermonkey
(coauthored with Phillip Robbins)

Eight Mules from Monterey

Jayhawker

Sarah and Me and the Lady from the Sea

Turn Homeward, Hannalee

For Jasmine (The Twig) Mortimer

Contents

1

Pressing herself flat against the rear wall of Señor Aguilar's hotel near the Avenida Ruiz, Lupita Torres bided her time. When she heard the doors of the big green *yanqui* car shut and the tourist start the engine, she slid forward, scraping her back on the rough white stucco. Sucking in her breath, Lupita nervously fingered the skirt of her faded cotton dress. Would the doorman shout at her not to hang around the elegant hotel?

Quickly Lupita stuck her head out and gave the front of the hotel a sweeping glance with her dark eyes. A sudden gust of hot September wind blew a lock of her long, black hair forward. She pulled it back, muttering in Spanish.

A second glance told her that the front entrance of the three-story Mexican hotel was deserted. *Bueno!* No one would catch her. The thin-legged thirteen-year-old moved swiftly around the side of the building to the iron steps that led to the higher floors. Her brown limbs flashing in the sunshine, Lupita ran up the steps past the first and second floors. Her hand twisted the knob of the third-floor door, and she slipped inside and stood in the middle of the long, gold-carpeted hallway.

¡Sí! Yes, there was her mother's cleaning cart down the corridor to the left. What a good job Mamá had as chambermaid in Señor Aguilar's hotel! Working here was much better than working in a bad-smelling fish cannery down on the bay of Ensenada.

Lupita moved warily toward the cart, noticing the mound of dirty sheets and used towels in the canvas hamper on one side and the array of neatly folded clean linen, bottles, and cans of cleanser below. Mamá probably was inside the room by the cart, number 310, changing the bed. She would be happy to see Lupita, who had just finished an errand in the neighborhood. Perhaps Mamá would permit her to help lift the big mattress and tuck the white sheet under it or polish the mirror in the glittering bathroom. How the tourists must delight in the gleam of metal and porcelain! What joy they must take in the wide, velvet-covered bed, the brick walls, and the heavy blue-green draperies Señor Aguilar provided for them.

"Mamá, it's Lupita Mañana," Lupita called out very softly, as she slipped inside and half closed the door behind her. Her mother was not in the bedroom. She must be in the bathroom, perhaps scrubbing the pink tub. Lupita called out again and walked over the shaggy royal-blue carpeting to open the bathroom door.

But her mother was not there either. Where was she then? Down the hall at the maid's closet, of course, getting more supplies. Lupita sighed. That's where she must go to find her even at the risk of discovery.

Perhaps a tourist might come out of a room and catch

her in the hall as had happened just last week. The sudden appearance of the *yanqui* in swimming trunks had frightened Lupita into statuelike stiffness. The tall, bald man, white as fish flesh, flicked a glance at her out of his queer, pale eyes, but he said nothing. After he looked at her, he continued on his way downstairs to the swimming pool Señor Aguilar maintained for his guests. The sea was too salty for them, said Mamá, when Lupita asked her about the man. Mamá laughed when Lupita described how fast he walked on his stiltlike legs and how jerky his movements were.

Lupita sucked in some air for courage and went out past the bed to the open door. There she looked out and listened. *Sí*, there was some noise from the linen closet, small sounds of someone moving around. Mamá!

Lupita went out into the hall, blessing the deep-pile carpet that covered the sound of her footsteps, and ran noiselessly to the maid's closet.

"Eh?" the woman there cried out softly, turning around. "Who is it?"

Lupita gaped at her. This woman was not her mother but Josefa, another chambermaid, the one who tended to the first floor. Plump, wrinkled Josefa looked at Lupita, who leaned against the wall. "*Sí*, it is Carmela's daughter, the one they call Lupita Mañana." She nodded as she put her hands into the deep pockets of the yellow-cotton coat all the hotel employees had to wear. "Is it true that you are called Lupita Mañana because when your father does not catch as many fish as he wants, you always say, 'Tomorrow, *mañana*, you will catch more, *Papá*?' "

"*Sí*, that is what I say. Where is my mother?"

"Ah, she has gone home. Señor Aguilar sent her home

when Captain Ortega's son came here to the hotel for her. I am doing your mother's work on this floor now."

Lupita felt a sudden stab of fright. Josefa doing her mother's work? The Torres family had to have the money her mother's job brought them. Had Señor Aguilar become angry about something Mamá had done and taken her job away? Had that long-legged tourist complained about seeing Lupita in the hall last week? And why had Captain Ortega, the captain of the tuna boat Papá worked on, sent his oldest son here to Mamá? The Ortega boat, *La Estrella*, must have come back to Ensenada from the fishing trip it had left on six days ago. Then Papá too was home again!

Lupita stammered, "Captain Ortega has come back?"

"Certainly Ortega is back," Josefa replied. "If Ortega sends his boy here, Ortega is back, foolish one."

"Señora, why did Mamá go home?" Lupita asked anxiously.

"I don't know. Who tells me anything? Señor Aguilar told me about the boy and your mother's going home. Then he ordered me to do the work up here, too." Josefa waved her hand. "Go home, girl, and find out. Do not pester me. I have much to do today." She added, grumbling, "Who knows when your mother will return?"

Not return? By now Lupita's heart had begun to hammer. Something had happened! Something was wrong! Forgetting to thank Josefa, Lupita whirled around and fled, racing down the iron stairs to the ground. "Go home," Josefa had said. *Sí*, that's just where she was going.

Lupita passed the dusty little park that had been built as a memorial to an assassinated *yanqui presidente*. On the other side she came up to a group of boys somewhat older than herself. They lounged against the wall of a liquor and soft-drink store, smoking cigarettes.

"*Hola*, Lupita Mañana," one of them cried out to her.

"Skinny, silly one," cried another, laughing.

This time Lupita didn't bother to call an insult to him. Instead she halted for a moment to gesture to a sulky-looking, black-haired boy, who was wearing an out-at-the-elbows mustard-yellow shirt, at the edge of the group.

"Salvador, come home now! Captain Ortega sent Paco to the hotel to get Mamá!"

"Captain Ortega? *Mamá*?" A look of quick interest transformed Salvador's face and then was followed by one of alarm. An instant later he was running beside her, asking, "Is it because of Dorotea?"

"I don't know, Salvador." Lupita panted. "I didn't see Paco. One of the other maids told me. She was doing Mamá's work. Something has happened! I know it has."

"*Sí!*" For once fifteen-year-old Salvador didn't argue with Lupita. He knew as well as she that only an emergency could take Mamá away from her job and perhaps cause her to lose her wages for the hours she was gone.

As they turned onto an even dustier, more littered road than the one the hotel was on, Lupita glanced at Salvador's face. She knew why he was worried. It was because of Dorotea Ortega, the captain's pretty fourteen-year-old daughter. Salvador hoped to make Dorotea his *novia*, his sweetheart, but Captain Ortega would not let him court her. The Ortega family was richer and more important than the Torres family. Captain Ortega did not want Dorotea to marry the son of Hernando Torres, who worked for him on his fishing boat. Ortega called Salvador a *vago*, a no-good, and had let it be known that

13

he wanted Salvador to keep away from his daughter. Even Paco Ortega, a friend of Salvador's, had warned him to leave Dorotea alone, and Dorotea had been warned by her parents to stay away from the Torres boy. But Salvador was in love and refused to listen to anyone. No one but Lupita knew that Dorotea met him secretly in town.

As they headed up a hill toward the Torres house, Salvador asked her, "Why did old Ortega send for Mamá, Lupita?"

"I do not know, Salvador. Perhaps somebody saw you with Dorotea and told the Ortegas. But then why shouldn't the captain talk with Papá not with Mamá?"

Salvador's dark eyebrows drew together in worry. "Maybe he wants to speak to both of them. Could someone have seen me kiss Dorotea Monday?"

The Torres' home was an old, pink-painted adobe building, which Lupita's father had enlarged with corrugated iron panels. Some scraggly pink geraniums, marigolds, and spindly poinsettia plants, Lupita's gardening efforts, bordered the front of the house. Usually when she came home from running errands for Ensenada shopkeepers for a few centavos, she stopped to admire her flowers. But not today. Today she didn't even see them.

Running behind Salvador, she rushed into the house past its three small guardians, her two little sisters and her five-year-old brother. They were standing outside the open door, the girls together as usual and the boy alone. All three looked solemn, frightened, and bewildered.

Sí, something had happened! Was Captain Ortega inside with Mamá and Papá, complaining to them about Salvador and Dorotea?

14

But there were no men at all in the dim room that served as the living room and kitchen. There were only Carmela García de Torres, Lupita's mother, and two neighbor women. Lupita's thin, small-boned mother was sitting in a chair, rocking back and forth, with one-year-old Hernando on her lap.

"*Ay de mí, ay de mí*, Hernando, Hernando!" she was wailing.

Lupita stared at the baby, who was crying, but not from sickness. She knew his cries, each and every one of them. Now he sounded irritated, not sick.

Lupita glanced at the neighbor women. One was the old, black-clad widow who took care of Hernando while her mother was at work. She hovered over Mamá, clasping and unclasping her bony hands. The other woman, who lived in the yellow house next to the Torres family, was lighting the little candle in the red glass cup. She set it before the picture of the Virgin Mary on the corner altar shelf between vases of pink paper roses.

"Mamá?" cried Lupita.

"Lupita!" Mamá opened her eyes. "Salvador, my son." She stopped rocking, gave the baby to the widow, and opened her arms to the two oldest of her six children.

"What is it? What is it?" asked Lupita, enfolded in her mother's embrace.

There came a torrent of gasping, choked weeping but no words save for, "Hernando, Hernando!"

"Papá? Papá? Is it Papá?" asked Salvador. "Tell me. Tell me."

"Salvador, Lupita." The black-clad neighbor put her hand on Lupita's shoulder. "Do you remember the windstorm and the rain we had three days ago?"

"Sí, sí, the *chubasco*." Lupita looked up at the woman, who was gazing at her out of mournful eyes. The wind had blown some tiles off the roof of Señor Aguilar's hotel.

The widow went on. "There was a storm out on the sea that night. *Ay de mí*, a great wave struck Captain Ortega's boat when your father was on deck keeping watch. The water took him with it when it passed over the boat."

As Lupita looked open-mouthed at the widow, the other woman, finished with the candle, came over to them. "The men looked for him in the sea, but they couldn't find him in the darkness and the rough water. Captain Ortega sent his boy to the hotel for your mother to come home so he could tell her. Afterward the captain told us what happened to your father, too."

Gradually the words sank into Lupita's awareness. Shrieking *"Papá!"* she buried her face in her mother's shoulder. Together they wept, and Salvador groaned aloud.

Hearing the wails of sorrow, the younger Torres children crept back inside the house and stood big-eyed against the wall under the Virgin's altar. They stared at their mother, Salvador, and Lupita. Then they looked at one another as if to ask, Why are they behaving so strangely?

Holding the baby in one arm, rocking him to stop his crying, the widow pointed to the three younger children. *"Pobrecitos,* poor little ones." She sighed. "What will happen to them now? It is very hard for children without a father when there is little money."

"Sí," the other woman agreed with a sigh. She nodded and confided, "But at least Carmela will not have to pay for her husband's funeral. His being swept into the sea

16

has saved her money she will need. *Ay de mí*, the sea, at least, has done that for her and the children."

For a time the baby wailed his thin cry, until finally Lupita got up from where she knelt and took him from the widow. "I will take him now. *Gracias*, thank you," she told the woman.

"It was nothing, Lupita. I like to hold him. I will go and get the priest for you now if you wish."

Her face streaked with tears, Lupita looked down at her baby brother, who had stopped crying the instant she had taken him and who was now sucking his thumb. What did he know of the tragedy that had befallen them? He was lucky not to understand.

"*Gracias*," Lupita said once more to the widow. "When Mamá is ready she will send Salvador for the priest. I will go to Uncle Antonio's and tell him."

With her heart silently crying her father's name, Lupita gazed accusingly at the candle-lit picture of the Virgin. How could my father die? she asked the picture silently. He was kind to us. He never drank too much in the *cantinas*. He always brought home all the money he earned on Captain Ortega's boat. He never smoked marijuana like some men or got in trouble with the police.

Everyone agreed that Hernando Torres had been a good husband and father. He took much notice of his children, not ignoring them as some other fathers did. He'd even permitted Salvador to keep a dog and Lupita a cat until the animals had died. And now he was lost to his family forever; a thing as simple and everyday as a wave in the sea had taken him from them.

Ay de mí, what would become of them now? The wages Mamá was paid at the hotel were too small to support the seven of them, and Lupita earned only centavos for her errands. Although he had tried hard, Salvador could find no work in Ensenada. He was too old to shine tourists' shoes or sell lottery tickets. Now that he'd quit school he roved about with a group of boys his own age, smoked cigarettes they gave him, and talked of automobiles and motorcycles, though no one owned one. Boast, strut, and smoke, that was all they did. The nearest Salvador had ever come to his dream of owning a car was to acquire an old rusting set of truck wheels, which he set tenderly behind the house. Not one of his friends brought home more than a couple of centavos a week to his family, but each and every boy came home to eat. *Ay de mí*, she was being too hard on them. It was not their fault they could find no work.

Lupita sighed as she looked from the Virgin's calm, smiling face to her yawning baby brother. The neighbor women were right in what they had said about Papá's death at sea saving them money. Mamá, Lupita knew, would have had to go to the moneylender to pay for a coffin and a new shirt.

Yet it would have comforted them all to see Papá in his coffin here in the house, with two candles at his head and two more at his feet. His friends and neighbors could have come to pay their last respects and for nine nights in a row say the rosary for him. Then she, who had been his favorite, would be able to take her marigolds, the flowers of the dead, to his grave on the special Day of the Dead. Lupita touched the little silver cross on its chain around her neck. It was her most precious possession, a gift from her father at her confirmation. Now it was doubly precious to her.

Again she asked herself what was to happen to them

now? Uncle Antonio had a sick wife, who went to the doctors all the time and required expensive medicine. He was not a rich man. The raw oysters he sold on the street were bought by poor Mexicans, never by rich *yanqui* tourists. No, Uncle Antonio could not help them, nor could the neighbors, who were as poor as the Torres family. Everyone who lived on the hillside around them was poor, some poorer than they.

What shall we do? Lupita asked herself for the third time, as she looked over her shoulder at her mother, who stared sadly at the three younger children lined up against the wall.

Salvador was standing beside Mamá. He had a look of pain on his face as if he had swallowed something that hurt him. Acting the part of a man, he'd refused to weep, but Lupita knew that he also mourned. *Ay de mí*, Salvador! He was the head of the family now, and he had no work. A man must have work!

What could she, Lupita Mañana, do?

2

As poor as they were, the two neighbor women cooked supper and brought it to the Torres house. They went back home after staying to say the first rosary with the grief-stricken family. Uncle Antonio, who had arrived earlier, stayed to speak to Mamá, and in a few minutes the young priest to whom Salvador had been dispatched came in.

Salvador remained in the room with the two men, standing against the wall as the guests and Mamá took the only three chairs. Lupita was sent out to put the younger ones to bed, first taking them out to the privy behind the house, then undressing them, and finally getting them into the big, old, sagging bed the three of them shared. Tonight she would sleep with Mamá and the baby in the brass bed, the best one in the room. Salvador, as always, would sleep on the cardboard he spread on the living-room floor.

Trying not to weep, Lupita tucked the sleepy children and the baby in for the night, telling her brother and sisters that Papá had gone up into the sky and become a star and that he would never come back to earth again. The girls nodded and asked no questions, while the boy only stared at Lupita. She added, "You can look up and see him. I will show you his star tomorrow night. He will watch over us."

"Sí, Papá will," agreed the little boy and closed his eyes.

Leaving the children, Lupita came back to the door, which she had left ajar. There she sat on a stool in the dark and listened to the voices in the other room. Mamá would not mind her doing that. What they said would matter to her, too.

Uncle Antonio, who talked a great deal, was speaking now. "So there will be Masses said in the church for my brother's soul and eight more nights of the rosary here. I can pay for the candles and for the Masses, too. And it is agreed that Salvador will go to Captain Ortega and ask him for my brother Hernando's place on his boat."

Lupita caught her breath, waiting for her brother to explode at the suggestion. As she'd expected, Salvador did. "No! I will not ask him! He would never have me."

The young priest's voice was soft. "Salvador, now that your father has died aboard Captain Ortega's boat, perhaps Ortega will favor you more. He had no insurance for his crew. He may feel he owes the Torres family something."

"No! Not him!" Salvador spoke in a harsh growl.

Mamá said, "Salvador, there is no harm in going to see Captain Ortega. The priest may be right."

"He isn't right," cried Salvador.

Lupita heard the sound of the front door closing behind someone. She peeked out into the living room. Had the priest felt insulted and left the house in disgust? No, he was still there with Mamá and Uncle Antonio. Salvador was the one who had gone out.

The priest asked, "Why does the boy not want to see the captain?"

"It is because of Captain Ortega's daughter, Dorotea," Mamá explained, with a deep sigh. "Ortega does not want his daughter courted by anyone but a rich man's son. He does not permit Salvador to see her, and Salvador does not. But he will not forget her."

Behind the door, Lupita shook her head. Mamá was wrong. Salvador had been seeing Dorotea secretly for months. She guessed that he had gone now to find Paco Ortega in town and talk with him. Salvador would be trying to get Paco to help him see Dorotea. *Ay de mí.* Lupita leaned her face wearily against the side of the door. Poor Salvador. He had two kinds of sorrow: the death of Papá and the trouble with Captain Ortega. Salvador had taken notice of several girls in town but slender, big-eyed Dorotea Ortega was the one he'd claimed as his sweetheart. She'd even given him a gift, a knife with the words "I die for love" inscribed on its blade. It was his most precious possession.

When Lupita came out in the morning to fix the family breakfast, beans piled into corn tortillas, she found Salvador asleep on the floor, rolled into a blanket.

Her mother, who'd wept half the night, was still in bed nursing the baby, so Lupita awakened Salvador and told him that food was ready.

As he got out of the blanket fully dressed, she said,

The money! Papá's money! Proud Salvador hadn't even asked for it. Lupita stepped forward, her heart hammering in her chest. She would have to ask for it then.

But she didn't need to after all. Captain Ortega shouted after Salvador, "Hey, *vago*, don't forget the money your father earned! Come back and get it."

The captain reached into his pocket and came nearer the wharf to throw a handful of pesos. The coins scattered over the mole. He laughed and bellowed, "Don't you want the money? Come back and pick it up."

Lupita stared after Salvador, who was a good distance away by now. She glanced at the laughing Ortega; then she knelt down and picked up all the pesos for which Papá had worked so hard. How fortunate none had fallen into the water beside the boat!

When she had them in her hand, she rose. Lupita stood for a moment, looking up into Captain Ortega's fierce, dark eyes; then she gazed past him at shamefaced Paco. No, she would not say *gracias* to the Ortegas. The money was Papá's. Squaring her thin shoulders and holding the money tightly, Lupita ran down the wharf after Salvador. Mamá would be happy to have the money; she didn't have to be told how badly Ortega had treated Salvador unless he himself chose to tell her.

At the end of the wharf, Lupita caught up with her brother. "I have Papá's money," she told him breathlessly.

He acted as if he had not heard her. "It wouldn't surprise me if the Ortegas bewitched Papá," he said angrily. "Dorotea's mother could have done it. She could have measured Papá with a black ribbon so he would die because she hates me. Lupita, I'm finished with all of the Ortegas, even Paco. If he comes near me again, I'll fight him."

29

"What of Dorotea, Salvador?"

He gave his sister a look of pain. "They will never let me see her again. She told me once if she could not marry me, she'd want to become a nun."

Lupita sighed. "Perhaps *mañana* will be better for you and her, Salvador."

Angry, scornful laughter burst from Salvador. "*Mañana, mañana, mañana*. Always it will be better tomorrow," he shouted at a shocked Lupita. Then he started to run, pounding toward the town.

After Lupita's supper of beans and rice that evening, Uncle Antonio arrived with other men to say the rosary for the second night. When the men had gone home, he remained to talk with Mamá and Salvador, and Lupita again was sent to put the smaller ones to bed. After she'd settled an argument about which star in the evening sky was Papá's, Lupita came back to sit by the half-open door.

She heard Mamá say in a queer, dull tone, "Sí, Antonio, you are right. *Ay de mí*! Shall I call Lupita in?"

"Sí, call the girl."

"Lupita, your uncle wants you."

Leaving her stool, Lupita came at once into the room and stood before her uncle.

"Tell her, Antonio," suggested Mamá.

Wizened Uncle Antonio with the drooping mustache said, "Lupita, your mamá and I talked this morning while you and Salvador were at Captain Ortega's boat. Then I spoke with a moneylender. He will lend her eight hundred pesos and will give her a year to pay it back before he takes this house. He is being very generous because he was a friend of your father's."

Bueno. Mamá was going to get some money then. Lupita was sorry, though, that she would have to borrow it.

"Lupita." Uncle Antonio cleared his throat. "Your mother cannot pay the moneylender back out of what she earns at Señor Aguilar's hotel and feed and keep you all, too. You and your brother Salvador must help her."

"I'll help her, Uncle Antonio. I'll do whatever I can."

He said softly, "Lupita, you and Salvador cannot earn enough money here in Ensenada, young as you are. So something must be arranged for you."

Lupita looked at Salvador. He had a very strange, shocked expression on his face. What was happening now?

"I could sell lottery tickets," she cried out. "I could get some piglets and raise them to sell, and I could keep hens for the eggs they will lay. I could sell oysters with you from your cart, Uncle Antonio. Perhaps I can even embroider for a shop. I can do many things."

"Those things will not bring in enough money. If you did all those things, Lupita, and Salvador found work, too, it would still not be enough to pay off the moneylender. You could not earn enough together to replace what my brother Hernando made on Ortega's boat."

Mamá explained, "It seems I must tell you what is arranged, Lupita. Most of the money I am to borrow is for you and Salvador. It is for you and him to go over there and find work."

Stunned, Lupita stared at her mother. "Over there?" No, it could not be! Her ears were playing her false.

"You two should go at once," Uncle Antonio said. "The day after tomorrow at the latest. Sí, you must go to the United States."

"The day after tomorrow?" Lupita echoed.

Mamá's tired eyes were full of tears. "Lupita, you and Salvador will go to your aunt Consuelo. You will write her a letter tonight and tell her you and Salvador are coming. With her help, you will surely find work and be able to send money to me. You must not impose on Consuelo, but earn your own way. She is in Indio, in California."

Lupita cried, "Where is Indio, Mamá?"

"I do not know. You must find it. I know only it is in the *gringo* state of California."

"How do we get to the United States?" Lupita asked frantically.

"I do not know that either. You and Salvador must find a way. I know that many others from Mexico have gone there." Mamá reached out and pulled Lupita to her, stroking her hair. "Do not tremble so, Lupita Mañana. Do not think that I want you and Salvador to leave me. But if we are going to live, you must go to California the way Consuelo went twenty years ago. It will hurt me if you and Salvador do not go willingly."

Lupita looked past her mother's arm at her brother, who was leaning back against the wall in his chair. He had taken out the knife Dorotea had given him and was staring at it. There was no expression on his face at all. "Salvador?" she said questioningly.

He looked up at her and answered sharply, "Mamá and Uncle Antonio are right. I'll go to this Indio, and I'll work there. I'll grow rich and send money home, and someday I'll come back here in an automobile, a big one like the *gringos* drive. Then I'll show everybody who Salvador Torres is!"

32

He was talking bravely just as she'd thought he would. Lupita said nothing, but her grief-bruised mind repeated, "Papá, Papá." First had come the great wave, then Captain Ortega's terrible unkindness, and now this dreadful blow: she must leave not only her family and town, but her country as well.

"Sí, sí, Lupita Mañana." Her mother patted her shoulder. "You will have Salvador to look after you. You will have your aunt Consuelo and her important husband to take care of you also. If only my two brothers had lived, they would help us now. So would my other sister if she was not a nun. Your father's sisters are in Loreto and as poor as we. Uncle Antonio has helped us as much as he can. Do not weep. You will come back here to Mexico, Lupita. It is not as if you will be gone forever."

Uncle Antonio gently added, "Many have gone over there. Entire families have gone. Many have been younger than the two of you."

Lupita held back the questions rising to her lips. Why had Aunt Consuelo never returned to Mexico? How many did they know who had come back?

Her mother tried to smile and looked into her daughter's eyes. "I have heard from waiters at the hotel that other families in Ensenada receive money from relatives who have gone to the United States to work. You and your brother are strong and clever. Consuelo will be pleased with you, and her *pocho* husband will see what fine Mexican children Hernando and I have." Her voice trailed off as she brought her apron up to her eyes.

When Uncle Antonio had left and Mamá had gone into the bedroom to nurse the baby, Lupita went over to Salvador, who was sitting in his chair.

"I know you, Salvador. You pretend you want to go away and come back rich so the Ortegas will be unhappy they did not let you marry Dorotea. You talk very bravely, Salvador, but I think you are afraid as I am also. Life is going to be strange over there. It is *yanqui* land, and they are different from us." Lupita clasped her hands. "Maybe they will not like us."

Salvador raised round, mournful eyes to meet his sister's. "Sí, I do pretend to want to go to please Mamá and Uncle Antonio. They spoke to me of our going before you came out. I've had some time to think." Salvador's voice dropped. "Lupita, we must go. We are the oldest. We must help Mamá get out of the hands of the devil who lends money. I know him. He was no friend to Papá. He is no friend to anyone. Yes, it will be strange over there and not easy. But something else will not be easy either."

Lupita looked at him. "What is that?"

Salvador shook his head slowly from side to side. "Lupita, you know nothing. You speak only with the family and other girls here in Ensenada, not with people who know important things. I must tell you that it is very difficult to cross over into the United States. They will not simply let us walk across and go to work."

"Why not?"

Salvador gripped one of her wrists. "Listen to me. I know that the *gringos* do not want us unless we have special papers from them that allow us to live there. I have heard men talk about that sort of thing. You and I can visit a short time as the *gringo* tourists visit here in Mexico, but the *gringos* do not want us to live and work in their country. We are not going to be welcome."

"Not even with Aunt Consuelo?"

"Lupita, all I know is that even if we can live with her and her *pocho* husband, we will be breaking the law."

"*Ay de mí*, we could go to jail over there," Lupita wailed softly.

"*Sí*, we could. Now you know." Salvador laughed his scornful laugh. "Now tell me that *mañana* will be better, Lupita."

3

Lupita lay beside her alternately sleeping and weeping mother for hours before she finally fell asleep near dawn. As she lay awake, she felt numb with the pressure of the evil things that had happened to her in so short a time. When she'd asked Mamá earlier if she and Salvador must leave so quickly, Mamá told her that Uncle Antonio had arranged to get the money from the moneylender first thing in the morning.

Lupita shivered, thinking of the moneylender. She knew him by sight, a sharp-nosed man with cold, small eyes. Sí, Mamá must pay him back on time. He would grab Papá's house in an instant and sell or rent it to somebody else. To make the payments, her mother must keep her job at the hotel and the next oldest girl could leave school and begin to sell lottery tickets. The other one could quit soon too and take care of the small boy and the baby. The widow would not be able to look after the baby once he began to run about. Lupita sighed. They would not get much schooling now, none of them. She had liked school and had grieved when Papa told her she must leave and start earning money by doing errands for people. Her dream had been to become a *profesora*, a teacher, someday, but she'd had to put that dream aside.

Listening to her mother's heavy breathing, Lupita sighed again. Could Salvador be right when he said the Ortegas had bewitched them? No, of course not. Lupita's teacher had told the class over and over that witchcraft was foolish superstition. Yet everything was falling into place to benefit the Ortegas, except for Dorotea, who must be sad too.

Perhaps Salvador could think of a way to send letters from the United States to Dorotea secretly. As for herself, she had already written the letter to Aunt Consuelo. It had gone to Consuelo Ruiz, Box 4, Route 2, Indio, California, USA. What a queer address. Lupita had copied it carefully from one of her aunt's old envelopes. What did the English words *box* and *route* mean? In any case, their meaning mattered little as long as the letter arrived, telling her aunt that Papá had been killed at sea and her niece and nephew were coming to Indio to find her. How hard it had been to write of Papá's death, far harder than to tell Aunt Consuelo that she and Salvador expected to find work in Indio. "Work hard" was how she had phrased it in the letter. Sí, she would work hard to help Mamá and the younger children. Mamá had said she was a good daughter. She would be a hard worker, too. Work would surely make her tomorrows better!

But, oh, how she would miss her family. Still, she would be with Salvador, not totally alone. She would have to look up to him now and obey him. He was not only two years older than she, he was almost a man and head of the Torres family. As such, he was the one to tell her what to do. She hoped, though, he would sometimes listen to advice from her. The teacher at school had asked her again and again to be a monitor in her classes. Didn't that mean she had a good head on her shoulders?

Uncle Antonio arrived soon after Lupita had fixed the customary bean-and-tortilla breakfast for everyone. He had gone to the moneylender, and now he handed the borrowed eight hundred pesos to her mother.

She counted out a hundred pesos and surprisingly handed the rest of the money not to Salvador but to Lupita. "Lupita," Mamá told her, "I must go to the church and speak with the priest about the Masses for your father, and then I have some other things to do. While I'm away, take Salvador's blue jacket, rip out an inside seam, put the pesos in there, and sew it up again so as not to show. You will wear that jacket and his old trousers and his red baseball cap. If you keep your braids up under the cap, no one will see them."

Startled, Salvador demanded angrily, "What? Lupita's to wear my clothing?"

"Sí, your uncle and I think it will be safer for her to travel as a boy. Salvador, you will wear your father's good coat and trousers. Lupita will sew the rest of the pesos save for a few you will carry in your pockets, inside that coat. You will leave tomorrow morning."

Lupita saw her brother's amazed glance and read his thoughts. He'd had time to ponder their forthcoming trip, and he'd decided he would rather go alone or, better yet, invite some friend to go along with him. Then the journey to the United States would become an adventure. Already Salvador was thinking of her as a burden.

Without a word, he hunched his shoulders and left the house.

Mamá excused his rudeness to Uncle Antonio. "Salvador has gone to say farewell to his friends. He is not himself. Forgive him."

Uncle Antonio nodded. "It does not matter. This is a hard thing for him." He smiled at Lupita. "It is a hard thing for you also, little one."

"Sí, it will be hard."

Lupita went into the bedroom where the family's clothing hung on nails. First she took down Salvador's blue jacket, then Papá's black-and-white checked coat. She held the coat to her cheek for a moment, wetting it with her tears, before she came out to the living room with Mamá's small sewing basket.

There was no one in the room when she entered except for baby Hernando, who was sitting on the floor, sucking his thumb. Outside her oldest sister was singing the same tune.

> *"Pon, pon, tata*
> *Mediecito pa la pa. . . ."*

Though it tore at her heart, Lupita at once started to sew. When Mamá returned that afternoon, she inspected Lupita's hiding place for the pesos. Then she and Lupita boiled a dozen eggs, which they packed into a small cloth bag along with some corn tortillas and a bottle of water.

"This food will take you and Salvador to Tijuana," Mamá instructed. "If you need more water, you can find it along the way. The priest told me so. This food will be your breakfast tomorrow morning. Do not forget the sack when you go away."

"No, Mamá." Lupita quickly looked away from her mother, fighting more tears. She had wept so much that her eyes and throat ached.

Mamá went on softly, "Lupita, leave early in the morning before the little ones awaken. I will tell them afterward why you and Salvador have gone. I do not want them crying all night long. As soon as the rosary is said for your Papá tonight, we shall all go to bed. You and Salvador must have some rest."

"Sí, I understand."

Lupita saw her mother bite her lip and then look suddenly away. "Sleep well if you can, Lupita. I'll give you my blessing in the morning."

When everyone went home that evening, Uncle Antonio again stayed behind. He embraced Lupita and said, "*Vaya con Dios*, little one. Go with God." Then he and Salvador went outside, where they talked for a long time.

At the first crow of the widow's cock, Lupita slipped out of bed. In the dark she struggled into a ragged old shirt of Salvador's, then his trousers, which she rolled up, and finally his blue jacket. She neatly tucked her long braids under his red baseball cap. The last thing she put on were her own leather sandals; his tennis shoes were too big for her.

"Lupita." Her mother's hoarse voice came from the dark bed. "Go now. I will pray for you. Do not make any noise as you leave. Write me from your aunt's house as soon as you have arrived. Now send Salvador in to me."

"Sí, Mamá." Lupita fumbled her way to her mother's side of the bed and bent over. She felt her mother's hands pull her down, and then she was kissing the tear-soaked face.

"*Vaya con Dios*, my daughter."

Lupita slipped out into the other room and went over to where her brother slept on the floor. He sat up. She could see by the dim light that he was fully dressed in Papá's clothing. Had he slept at all? "Lupita?" he whispered.

"Sí. Mamá wants to bless you, too. Go to her now."

Salvador said nothing, but he got up and went softly into the bedroom. Lupita folded his blanket and put both it and the cardboard he'd slept on under the table. When she heard her brother's quick, returning footfalls, Lupita picked up the sack of food she had left on the chair beside the front door the night before.

Salvador grunted, "Come on then," and they stepped out the door into the dawn.

Closing the door silently after her, an exhausted, dry-eyed Lupita followed Salvador down the hill into the town. "Go with God," Mamá and Uncle Antonio had told her. Lupita looked up at the sky where a few late stars winked down at her. She wished she could believe that one was Papá's and that wherever she went he would look down on her and bless and protect her. But that was only a pretty thought, made up for small children, who would believe anything anyone told them.

Lupita thought of calling out to Salvador to slow his pace, but she did not. Let him go through Ensenada ahead of her if he so chose. He was trying to show his courage by being her leader. Let him then. He needed to. When they passed through town, she could catch up with him. She'd point out to him then that she was supposed to be a boy too and that he should behave toward her as if she were one.

Some dogs barked at them as they went along the

41

paved road leading north out of Ensenada, but that was the only attention they received. Crowing roosters and yapping dogs were the only creatures abroad at dawn today. In a little while the town would start to come alive, and the fishing boats would sail out of the bay into the ocean. Perhaps Captain Ortega had already prepared *La Estrella* for another expedition, with a new man aboard to replace Hernando Torres. Lupita felt sure that Ortega wouldn't find anyone as good as Papá had been. Despite his feelings about Salvador, Ortega had kept Papá on his crew. That proved Papá was one of the best fishermen in port.

At the north edge of town, just below the rich Chapultepec hills district, Lupita ran up to her brother with a tortilla and an egg taken from her sack.

As they both ate, she asked, "How far is it to the United States?"

"It is two or three days' walk to Tijuana. That is where the border is." He grunted and added, "I do not know how far it is in distance. Perhaps later we can get a ride in an automobile."

"An automobile, Salvador?"

"*Sí*, an automobile, silly one," he mocked her. "Why should we walk if we can ride? I'll call out to a car when we see one."

"Mamá and Uncle Antonio did not tell us to get rides in cars."

Salvador laughed harshly. "They did not tell us not to either. I'll keep watch for a Mexican car. No *gringo* would pick us up, and if he did, how could we talk to him unless he spoke Spanish? One of my friends went to Tijuana once. He got a ride in the back of an old truck driven by a Mexican. He was lucky. The truck went almost all the way into Tijuana."

Lupita looked back at Ensenada, which lay under a soft, white mist that had drifted in from the sea.

"Don't look back," Salvador ordered her sharply. "Keep your eyes ahead, and don't weep. Remember, you're a boy, my brother not my sister. Walk beside me, and do as I do."

"I won't cry, Salvador." Walking beside him, she slipped her hand into his.

He angrily jerked his away, but then a few steps later he reached out and took her hand for a moment in his again.

They walked along the paved road together, and after a time Salvador pointed out the Todos Santos Islands offshore. Papá had sailed among them, and he had often spoken of them to Lupita. They were beautiful but had no fresh water, so only sea lions and seabirds lived there. Lupita could spy some pelicans out fishing, diving awkwardly into the sea. How they plummeted straight down into the water! One would think they would be hurt by their furious impact with the sea, but, no, they almost always came up with a fish in their beak. The pelicans worked hard to satisfy their needs. They thrived by effort. Why shouldn't she and Salvador?

As she walked along the rising road that bordered the sea, Lupita's eyes smarted from the sharp brightness of the blue water and the white surf curling onto the beach many feet below. The sea was peaceful now, sunny and radiant. Looking at it below, she could hardly believe that it had been so cruel as to sweep Papá away. It could not be trusted.

43

Lupita let out a deep sigh of sadness, asking herself if even the effectiveness of hard work could be trusted. Who knew what working in *yanqui* country would be like? If only she or Salvador knew the language, they would have an easier time.

"Lupita, do not sigh so much," chided Salvador. "Boys don't do that. If you feel sad, curse but don't sigh. Curse old Ortega if you want to. Call him every bad name you can think of."

"*Sí,* Salvador."

As midmorning arrived, several big, gleaming tourist cars and a bus traveling south to Ensenada passed them. Going fast on the good road, they whizzed by, the people inside not even glancing their way. Three older-model cars with Mexican license plates went by in the other direction, but none stopped at Salvador's signal. A green bus half full of Mexicans passed them next. When it had gone by, Salvador said, "I wish Mamá had told us to ride a bus."

"It would cost money we might need later," Lupita warned. "Perhaps the next car going north will pick us up."

"Always Lupita Mañana!" Salvador muttered.

The next car, a banged-up red sedan, went past them in a cloud of exhaust fumes.

Salvador looked down at his sister and repeated, "*Mañana, mañana.*"

But all at once the red car made a U-turn and returned, stopping a distance ahead of them. A thickset young man in a plaid shirt got out of the passenger side and gestured for Salvador and Lupita to come up to the car.

"They want us! Come on," Salvador said, and they both began to run.

By the time they were at the car, the driver had got out too. Also young, he was tall, thin, and wore a high-crowned, straw cowboy hat.

When Salvador and Lupita reached them, the tall one asked with a grin, "Are you going to Tijuana?"

"*Sí*," replied Salvador eagerly.

"And you want a ride, eh?" asked the heavyset one.

"*Por favor.*"

"Are you hoping to cross the border there?" The tall one stepped nearer to Salvador.

When Salvador made no reply, the heavyset Mexican chuckled and told his companion, "Of course, they plan to do that!"

The driver laughed. "Then you must have money with you."

"No, we do not have money!" Salvador stepped backward, alarmed, while Lupita stood behind him, frozen with terror.

The tall youth moved very swiftly. He hit Salvador in the face with his fist, caught him before he could fall, spun him around, and pinioned his arms behind his back.

"Salvador!" Lupita shrieked.

"Ramón, look to the little one's pockets. I'll tend to this one," ordered the tall fellow.

Ramón, who stank of liquor, grabbed hold of Lupita's throat and held her tightly, but not so tightly that she couldn't breathe. Terrified that the baseball cap might fall off and reveal her braids, Lupita didn't resist as he reached down with his other hand and pulled out the pocket linings of the jacket she wore.

"Nothing here!" he called to his companion.

"The bigger kid's got four pesos, that's all. Let the little one go."

Whereupon, Ramón gave Lupita a push that threw her on the roadside. A moment later the tall fellow hit Salvador with an open-handed blow to the side of his head. "Ramón, see what's in the sack the little one's got with him," he ordered.

From her place on the gravel-strewn ground, a trembling Lupita watched Ramón peer into the sack of food she'd dropped when he'd pushed her. Thanks to the Virgin Mary, these robbers had not found the money sewn into their clothing or discovered that she wasn't a boy. But would they steal their food?

Ramón dropped the sack beside Lupita. "Tortillas and eggs and a bottle of water. That's all they have," he said with disgust. "Do you want the eggs or tortillas? I don't."

"No, leave it all. We can do better than that." The tall youth chuckled as he stuffed Salvador's pesos into his shirt pocket. "*Estupidos*, stupid ones," he sneered at Salvador and Lupita. "You'll never get across the border. You'll starve to death in Tijuana."

Then he tilted his hat farther forward, got in the car, waited for Ramón, and drove off with a roar.

Lupita was on her feet first. "Salvador, Salvador," she cried softly, leaning over her brother. "Did he hurt you?"

Salvador sat up, rubbed his jaw, and felt his head. "Not much, but my jaw aches and so does my head."

"Shall I help you get up?"

"No."

He got to his feet, and with clenched fists he stared after the red car still in sight farther up the highway. First, he cursed the robbers and their fathers and mothers. Then he said, "He didn't take Dorotea's knife. He didn't look in my belt."

"And, Salvador, they didn't find the other pesos. *Salvador!*" He was still staring angrily up the road. Lupita tugged at his sleeve until he glared down at her. "Please, Salvador, I do not want a ride to Tijuana. It would be better to walk. When we hear a car coming, we can hide."

Rubbing his bruised jaw again, Salvador only nodded as Lupita fell into stride beside him, and they once more started on their way northward.

She stole a glance at his face as they walked along. It was sullen with helpless fury at all the bad luck that had befallen them lately. But at least Salvador still had his knife, something that meant as much to him as Papá's silver cross did to her. Though Lupita could never tell him, she wouldn't have been sorry if it had been stolen too. It might be protection for them, but it could also get Salvador and herself into much trouble in Tijuana and over there. She remembered something she'd once overheard Papá say to Uncle Antonio. Papá had not liked Dorotea Ortega's gift to his son. He had said that a boy who carried a knife on his body carried the thought of using it in his head.

All at once Salvador spoke. "If they had got all the money, we would have had to go back, Lupita. We must see to it that no one ever robs us again. We are fortunate to have my knife. There may be robbers over there also. I am sure there will be."

Ay de mí, Lupita told herself. Papá had been right. The knife was on Salvador's mind more than ever now.

4

Much to Lupita's relief, Salvador didn't hail any more automobiles that day, and none stopped for them. Lupita was ready to run inland if any did. They sat down twice to eat on rocks beside the road. Behind them, a mile or so away, mountains rose up to a sharp blue sky.

At their second stop, Salvador warned her, "Be careful. Watch for scorpions under the rocks and for *víboras*, rattlesnakes, lying on top of them."

"Sí, Salvador," Lupita replied. Then she asked, "Where shall we stop tonight to sleep? Can we find a place that will be safe?" Thinking of the robbers, she added, "I had not thought our own people would rob us."

Salvador laughed. "No? If a person has money, anyone will rob him, *tonta*, fool!"

At sunset, they came across a ruin of a half-finished concrete-block building. It was surrounded by high weeds and cacti, and inside some wild pigeons roosted. "Here! We will sleep here," Salvador announced, after he had scouted a small room for scorpions or tarantulas. "We will sleep in the corner over there." He pointed to the corner nearest the door.

"What if someone comes here tonight?"

Nodding, he pointed to another door leading out to the back of the ruin. "There are two doors. We can go out the other one then. Now lie down and sleep, Lupita."

Lupita lay down with the sack of food between herself and the wall, and Salvador lay down beside her.

"I wish we had a blanket," she said wistfully. "Should we make a fire?" There were matches inside the food sack too.

"You don't need blankets in September. Go to sleep. A fire could bring someone here. Perhaps we will hear coyotes, but pay no attention. They won't come in here. If one does, I will shout at him."

"Salvador?" Lupita moved closer to her brother. "Salvador, was I brave? Did I do well when the robbers came?"

"Sí, I was not ashamed of you. Put your head on my shoulder if you want to, but do not weep."

"No, Salvador."

Lupita, shivering in the nighttime breezes that came in with the fog from the ocean, heard coyotes howling that night, but none came to the ruin. In the morning, she and Salvador ate more eggs and tortillas and drank some of the water in the bottle. The bottle was almost empty by now. Walking was a thirsty business.

When he saw Lupita's worried look, Salvador said, "We'll get more water at Rosarita Beach. Remember, Uncle Antonio said we would be sure to get some there if not before."

Once more they took to the road, walking north toward

the United States border. Again they did not seek rides and no one stopped to offer one, although many cars passed them. The sun grew so hot on their backs that both took off their jackets and carried them. Lupita was glad of Salvador's baseball cap; it kept off some of the heat. Both she and Salvador complained of their sore feet.

They made faster time than Salvador had expected, and they walked into Rosarita Beach with the morning only half gone. The town was much smaller than Ensenada, but it had a few hotels, stores, and service stations. At one of them, Salvador asked the man who was pumping gas to let him fill the water bottle from his hose.

"Sí," the Mexican told him, as he examined Salvador and Lupita out of the corner of his eye. When they left, he gave them a crooked grin and shook his head, but said nothing.

Across the highway and walking north again, Lupita said, "I think that man knew where we were going and what we want to do."

"It does not matter, Lupita, as long as he does not rob us too."

Some miles farther on, they took a road running inland, away from the sea. Before she turned onto it, Lupita stopped and looked back at the ocean she'd known all her life. In the late afternoon, it was purplish blue beneath a flaming golden sun. She murmured, "Papá, Papá," then spun about and ran to catch up to Salvador.

As they approached Tijuana, they saw more and more automobiles of varied colors, shapes, and sizes. When the cars passed them, they created gusts of wind that Lupita felt as blows on her body. Some five miles from the city, she spied an enormous circular building, a stadium where bullfights took place.

By the time the bullring was out of sight behind them, it was dusk. As they walked along the highway, some cars came perilously close, as if the drivers were playing a cruel game with them. Over and over, she and Salvador jumped onto the roadside. While Lupita prayed, Salvador cursed and shook his fist at the disappearing cars.

It was full dark when they came into Tijuana, walking beneath the steep hills on the right side of the road. Lights twinkled around them. People lived on hills here, too, as they did in Ensenada.

Salvador refused to gasp at his first view of Tijuana's central district, but Lupita stood awestruck. Never had she seen so many lights! White, red, green, and yellow neon signs—all blinking and flashing. The shopwindows were alight, filled with displays of gleaming silver or leather goods. Never had she heard so much noise! Street vendors were shouting their prices; drivers were honking their horns, trying to get other drivers out of their way; cars were squealing to a stop at red traffic lights and then roaring off again at the green ones. The loud, bouncy music of trumpets and guitars came at her from every direction. Every shop they passed blared music. The street was crowded with people, Mexicans and Americans, more *gringos* than Lupita had even seen before. There were young ones and middle-aged ones and even old ones, *gringos* all, with yellow hair and light brown hair and even hair as red as chili peppers. One, a young woman, pointed at Lupita as she and Salvador stopped to stare at a winking nightclub sign of bright pink and red lights. The *gringa* spoke to her companion, a man her own age, and then they both chuckled. Lupita became afraid. What was this woman saying? Was she about to make trouble for her and Salvador?

She reached out for her brother's hand but could not find him by her side. Where was Salvador? He had been there only an instant before. Where had he gone? Lupita looked about her frantically for Papá's black-and-white coat. Ah! There was Salvador, standing a distance away from her, looking at something on the wall of a building.

Running over to him, she gazed up too. Her cheeks flaming, Lupita looked down at the sidewalk. There was a color photograph of a long-haired woman, wearing a red spangled costume that covered even less of herself than the bathing suits the *gringa* tourists wore in Señor Aguilar's swimming pool. To her horror, she read the name over the picture, "Lupita Lasso." Her name!

"She dances in there." Salvador gestured to the half-open door of the theater.

Lupita looked directly at his face, not the shameful photograph, and said, "Salvador, we must find a place to sleep. My feet are very sore. I cannot cross over the border tonight."

Salvador turned away from the photograph and said with a laugh, "Her name is Lupita too. All right, I won't look anymore. She's old, anyway. My friend who was here in Tijuana says there is a park. He told me it was not far from the place they play the game of jai alai. That is where he slept when he was here."

"Will it be safe there?"

"He said the police come there so often to inspect that he found it hard to sleep at all."

"*Bueno*. I am tired." Lupita took hold of her brother's hand and held it tightly as they stepped off the sidewalk's high curb and waited in the street for the traffic light to change. Her heart beat fast as they crossed the Avenida Revolución, Tijuana's most important street. This city with its hundreds of automobiles, flashing lights, crowds, and noise frightened her. Would it be like this over there, too? Would Indio, California, be like Tijuana?

Arriving at the park early, Salvador and Lupita found an empty bench. They lay down on it together and tried to sleep, but they got very little rest. Men and boys, looking for a place to sleep, prowled all night. Then came the police with flashlights, searching for troublemakers. Lupita awoke three times, startled, by a light shining on her and Salvador. Satisfied by the sight of the two boys, the police moved on through the park.

Just before dawn a cramped and aching Lupita listened in spite of herself to the conversation of the two men sitting on the bench to her right. They were talking about the war, and she could tell from their voices that they were *viejos*, old men.

One said, "It was forty years ago, the great *yanqui* war. That was when we were invited to go over there and work in their fields. The *gringos* took us in buses, and they kept us in houses and fed us. We were called *braceros* then, and we made much money. Those were good days."

"Do you hope to go over there again?" the other asked.

"*Sí.*" The man laughed in the dark. "Who does not hope to go and make much money? Do you?"

"No, I am too old now. I have no family over there. Do you?"

"*Sí*, a son and two nephews. I will go *mañana* to visit them, and then in three days I will come back."

"You will not try to find work?"

"No." He chuckled. "I am far too old to sneak over. That is too hard for an old man like me. Do you want a cigarette?"

"Sí. I know what you mean. It is indeed too hard for *viejos* like ourselves."

The conversation ended when both began to smoke, but Lupita stored what they had said in her memory. Salvador had been correct in thinking that getting into the United States to work would be difficult. It would be different if they were going only to visit. These two old men had confirmed what her brother had told her. *Ay de mí*, she had hoped he would be wrong!

Breakfast in the park consisted of the final two tortillas and eggs and the last of the water. Lupita stuffed the bottle into the sack with the matches and put it into her jacket pocket.

"Let's go to the border now," Salvador told her. "We can see what goes on there."

Obediently Lupita arose and followed him out of the park. There were no flashing neon signs in Tijuana by day, but the music still blared from the shops. After Salvador asked directions of a small boy, they crossed the Avenida Revolución and turned onto the Boulevard Cuahtenoc. Then they crossed over the dry bed of the Tijuana River onto a road that led past the district called the Colonia Libertad. Early as it was, a stream of cars headed in the same direction. As the two approached the border, they saw that many of the automobiles had parked. People were getting out of them and walking along the roadway and sidewalks.

"*Ay de mí.*" The expression of dismay burst from Lupita as she looked at the border checkpoint. A high metal fence stretched along each side of the border, and a large building was set in the middle. Through the building's glass windows she could see people standing in lines. She could also see men in green and tan uniforms, Mexican and *gringo* guards standing together.

As she and Salvador stood back, studying the building and fence, Lupita noticed that other people were also staring at the fence. None of them went forward, although other men and women passed by, chattering of visiting in San Diego and Los Angeles.

Lupita edged nearer Salvador. "Do you know a way to cross over?"

"No, not yet. We just arrived here, remember?" He gave her an annoyed look. "We'll go back into Tijuana and ask around. People there must know many ways."

"Salvador, we have eaten all of our food."

"Buy more. We can find a shop that sells food."

On the way back to the center of Tijuana, Lupita ducked into an alley and opened a seam of her jacket. She took out some pesos, which she handed to her brother, and then she pinned the seam back together with a safety pin. At the first grocery store that they passed, she bought a box of crackers and a can of refried beans, which the shopkeeper opened for her. That would feed them for two days, Lupita estimated. She put the food carefully into the cloth sack, and then the two of them went out into the Avenida Revolución. For all his pretended bravery, Lupita saw that Salvador was too shy to ask anyone how to cross the border. Everyone moved so fast and with so much purpose here, not the way they did in Ensenada. Even the midday *siesta* time spent in the park seemed shorter than at home.

Though footsore from their long journey, Lupita and Salvador investigated Tijuana's major streets from one end to another. What things they saw. Women selling bunches of great orange, yellow, and scarlet paper flowers; men selling *menudo*, a spicy tripe dish, from a cart; even a wild-haired fire-eater, who took a swallow of alcohol, put a lighted torch into his mouth, and blew red flames toward the passersby. Fearing that her baseball cap would ignite, Lupita clutched it to her head, turned, and ran away. The fire-eater, amused, yelled at Salvador to catch his little brother before he ran south all the way to Mexico City.

Afterward they wandered past another bullring to Calle Numéro Uno and Calle Tercero, always looking for someone who seemed friendly and who might have the time to talk with them.

Suddenly, on Calle Tercero, Salvador stopped in his tracks as he walked ahead of a weary, lagging Lupita. He stood rooted in front of a shopwindow. What interested him so much? Lupita caught up to him, and she gasped aloud at what she saw. A hat! A *charro* hat, big and wide, glistening with gold and silver braid. Beneath this magnificent hat lay a pair of silver spurs with huge gold-plated, star-shaped rowels. Lupita heard her brother sigh, and she nodded. When Salvador had been a little boy, he had been greatly taken with the *charros*, who rode such fine horses in the parades in Ensenada on fiesta days. He had dreamed of being a *charro* himself someday. But *charros* were not poor cowboys but rich men, and Salvador had learned that he, a fisherman's son, could never become one. His desires had moved to motorcycles and cars, but Lupita could see that the glamorous *charro* still held a place in his heart.

As he went on gazing at the hat and spurs, a small man

with a large mustache came out of the shop to lounge against the doorjamb and grin at them. "You like the *charro* hat, *muchachos*, eh?" he asked them in a friendly way.

"*Sí*," breathed Lupita, pleased at being taken for a boy.

Salvador pointed north and asked, "Are there any *charros* over there, *señor*?"

The man shook his head. "Not like there are here in Mexico. I've been there many times and have never seen a *charro*." He asked casually, "Aren't you going over there, *muchachos*?"

"No," Salvador told him flatly.

"Don't you want to go and see the sights?"

Remembering the robbers on the road, Lupita stiffened and moved back, but Salvador answered, "*Sí*, my little brother and I would like to see what is over there."

"Why don't you go then?"

Salvador asked quickly, "Señor, how does one get over there?"

"To work?" asked the man.

After a moment, Salvador said, "To work."

The shopkeeper nodded, gazed at the fine hat, and said, "It can be arranged, *muchachos*. Do you have someone to go to in the United States?"

"*Sí*."

"*Bueno*. That will make it easier for you. Come inside to talk." His eye fell on Lupita. "Don't be afraid. I am not going to hurt you. I can help you."

"Who are you? What is your name?" she asked.

"I am Señor Diaz. My cousin Tomás is the man you wish to see, not me. Lucky for you, he is here now behind my shop. Come along."

57

"Come on," Salvador ordered. He and Señor Diaz stepped inside the shop, which sold items that *charros* might buy such as jackets, ruffled shirts, whips, and elegant riding boots. Lupita trailed the two of them, trying to behave with courage.

Señor Diaz walked through a set of red curtains into a small back room where a man sat playing a solitary game of cards. He didn't resemble the shopkeeper at all. He was fat almost to the point of roundness, clean-shaven, and had a merry-looking face with small, twinkling eyes.

"What have you brought in here today?" he asked Diaz with a chuckle.

"Two boys who want to cross the border, Tomás."

"Eh?" The fat man gave Salvador and Lupita the once-over. Then he asked, as he slapped down one card atop another, "*Muchachos*, have you got a place to go to over there?"

"*Sí*," Salvador said.

"*Bueno.* Is someone expecting you?"

Lupita thought of the letter to Aunt Consuelo. She was sure her aunt had not received it yet. "No, not yet," she answered.

He sighed. "You cannot go over there on credit if there is no one there ready to pay for you. So you must pay me now for your forged papers and to guide you across." Tomás held all the cards in one pudgy hand while he stared at Lupita out of eyes that were no longer merry. "Here in Tijuana we use *gringo* money, dollars, as often as we use pesos. To take you over the border with me, I want two hundred dollars from each of you. That comes to around four thousand pesos."

"Four thousand pesos!" stammered Salvador.

"*Sí*, that is what I ask and so do the others who help people cross the border." The fat man spoke to his cousin. "These boys have no money. Get rid of them. Do not bring me children. When I go over tonight, I want to take adults with me not children." Tomás waved his hand. "Go away, *muchachos*. You cannot hope to cross the border without a guide. Hundreds try every day and get caught. Go back where you came from."

Lupita didn't wait to be ordered out again. Whirling around, she fled through the curtains and out through the shop into the sunlit street. Salvador stalked angrily behind her.

"Salvador!" she cried, but he grabbed her by one shoulder and put his hand over her mouth.

"Be quiet," he hissed into her ear. "Don't cry. Let's get away from here to where we can talk alone."

At Lupita's nod, he let go and both of them walked hurriedly down the street and around the corner into a littered alley. There Salvador halted.

In a whisper he told Lupita, "I think that Tomás is as big a robber as those two on the road. If we had four thousand pesos, I wouldn't give him one of them, not a centavo. Did you hear him say he was crossing over with people tonight?"

"*Sí*, I heard him. I did not like his little eyes."

Salvador nodded. "Lupita, think. Why can't we be with him then? We'll watch him all day long. I'll stay in front of the shop across the street, and you stay in back here. When he leaves, we'll follow him."

"What if he gets into an automobile, Salvador?"

"Even then we must find a way to follow him."

5

After Salvador left to go around the corner to take up his post, Lupita walked down the alley till she stood across from the *charro* shop. She recognized its rear entrance by the name painted above the door. In back of her was a deep-set doorway not in use. Boards in the shape of the letter X had been nailed across the door. There was space under the X for her to crawl in and sit down with her back to the door and her knees drawn up to her chest. Sticking her head out above the center of the boards, she could see anyone in the alley. She hoped Salvador had found as good a hiding place on the Calle Tercero.

Hours went by, but Lupita scarcely moved. Her hips ached from her cramped posture. She had just tilted the water bottle to her mouth when she saw a truck, a new-looking black pickup, come around the corner. It screeched to a halt in back of Señor Diaz's shop. A young, long-haired Mexican, wearing a red scarf headband and a yellow vest, got out. With the car keys jingling in his hand, he went into the shop.

A moment later he was back in the alley, and Tomás was with him. Under her breath, Lupita hissed, "*Gordo,*" fat one. Tomás was angry with the young man. She could tell by the expression on his face and the movements of his hands that he was giving him a tongue-lashing.

Then Tomás and the youth walked around the truck to the front and halted there. The older man pointed, stabbing a finger at the left front fender. Lupita saw the cause of his anger now. The fender was dented and crumpled. The young man had been driving the truck and had had an accident with it. He had told Tomás about it, and Señor Tomás was *very* angry. This automobile must belong to him then! Why else would he become so angry? What would happen next? Would he strike the young man?

No. Tomás stuck out his hand, palm upward, and the young man dropped the car keys into it. Tomás put them in his pocket and, glaring at the young man, jabbed his thumb toward the rear door of the shop. Then both of them went inside.

For a time Lupita waited. Then she crawled out of the doorway and ran down the alley to the street. She found Salvador sitting on the edge of the high curb, talking with a younger boy.

When he saw her, he got up, said, "*Adiós,*" to the boy, and came to her.

Lupita said softly, "Salvador, fat Tomás has a truck in the alley behind the shop. I know it is his. He has the keys to it."

"*Sí.*" Salvador nodded. "I saw the truck go by not long ago. It is a new black one. Is anybody in the alley now?"

"No."

"*Bueno.* Let's go see that fat coyote's car."

61

As they started to walk, Lupita turned and asked, "Coyote?"

"That is the name for men who take people over the border. The boy told me. This Tomás, he is the fattest coyote in Tijuana."

"Has that boy been over there himself?"

"Not yet, but he hopes to go. He does not have enough money to pay a coyote either. Each year they ask for more money."

Before Lupita and Salvador entered the alley, they looked carefully up and down to make sure that no one else was there. When they were satisfied, they went as far down as the black pickup truck. Salvador stepped silently up onto the running board and peered over the side. Lupita watched him anxiously. Suddenly she saw him reach over into the back, and then she heard a series of popping sounds. What was Salvador doing?

"Lupita," he hissed, and he gestured for her to give him the sack of food.

Taking it from her, he leaned over and put it inside. Then he held out his right hand. She took hold of it, jumped onto the narrow running board, and looked down into the back of the truck.

Now she understood what the popping sounds were. Over the bed of the truck was a protective canvas cover that was closed by grip fasteners. Salvador had opened several on the left side.

"Get in," he told her, taking her by the hips and pushing her upward over the left rear fender.

Get in this fat coyote's truck? She gave her brother a beseeching look, but he only pushed harder. Obediently Lupita climbed up over the fender and lay down on the metal bed of the truck. A minute later Salvador lay next to her. He reached up and snapped the fasteners shut once more.

He said grimly, "From now on we go where that coyote goes."

Lupita looked around her and saw nothing but a spare tire and some tools. "What shall we do in here?" she asked.

"Wait. Wait and keep quiet."

"*Sí*. Are you hungry, Salvador?"

At his nod she gave him the water, opened the cracker box, and scooped out some beans for both of them.

"You did well to come tell me about the truck."

"*Gracias*, Salvador." His words of praise warmed her.

Through eating, Lupita put the precious food back into the sack. She lay on the hard, hot metal with Salvador and looked up at the queer canvas.

Though they could breathe, they soon found themselves panting from the heat of the afternoon sun beating down on the canvas above them. It was dusk by the time Lupita heard the rear door of the shop open. She heard Tomás speak.

"*Adiós*, Diaz. See that that *tonto* son of mine doesn't give you any trouble in your shop. Tell him to go home in time for his supper. Let him walk. I'll be home by ten o'clock. Call my wife and tell her, *por favor*."

"*Sí. Adiós*, Tomás."

Lupita felt the balance of the truck shift as the *gordo* got inside. Then the engine started, and the pickup began to move.

Lupita whispered, "This coyote did not look to see what might be in his truck, the Virgin be praised!"

"Why should he look under the cover?" Salvador laughed, a hollow, soft laugh. "Hang on now so you don't get hurt, Lupita."

What a bumping, bruising ride there was for the two of them as Tomás drove toward his unknown destination. As he twisted and turned the car through Tijuana, Lupita could hear noise and she could even see the dim colors of the traffic lights overhead through the canvas.

Then came darkness and silence except for the sound of the truck's motor. It seemed to Lupita that they were climbing.

She had no idea how far they had traveled or where they were when Tomás brought the truck to a halt. He turned off the engine and got out, shutting the door softly. Lupita held her breath. What was going to happen now?

At first there was the sound of the wind only. Then Lupita heard soft voices speaking Spanish. There were men's voices and women's too. Over them rose the voice of Tomás. "All is ready. I know a path through these hills. Follow me."

"Don't we ride over in your truck?" asked an old man's voice.

"No, there is no road for a truck. We must walk, and you must follow me closely. Do not lose sight of me until I turn you over to the *gringos*. They will take you to a place they know."

Salvador crawled over to the side of the truck bed and opened the snap fasteners. Lupita sucked in her breath. Would the coyote hear? No. Salvador managed all very cunningly.

"Lupita," he whispered, "wait till they all leave with him. Then we'll follow."

Crouched, Lupita waited, while Salvador watched the Mexicans leave with Tomás. At his signal, she followed him over the side of the truck to the ground. "Come on," he called softly. "I see them. Hurry. Hurry!"

With only a glance upward at the star-spangled sky and the trees twisting in the wind, Lupita ran after her brother. She, too, could see the black shapes of the half dozen people ahead of them.

For a time the path they followed climbed; then it reached the crest of a hill and began to descend. Descend to where? Had they crossed the border into the United States? There was no fence to be seen. Didn't that tall fence at the border checkpoint run along the entire bottom of the United States? Had they gone through a wide gap someone had cut in it, a hole so big she could not see it? Could they still be in Mexico?

Lupita was still wondering where she was when she heard a very loud whirring sound. It froze her to the spot. The sound came from directly overhead. As she glanced to see what it was, an enormous shaft of brilliant white light stabbed her in the eyes. Red lights glittered in the sky too. She had seen the thing above them in Ensenada once. It was a helicopter, hovering, shining its searchlight down on them. It must be the police, the *guardia,* but up in the sky!

"Lupita, come on!" Salvador shouted.

She looked and saw him in the white light. For the first time, she could make out the others in the coyote's party. Including Tomás, there were eight of them. All were hurrying, stumbling forward down the hill as fast as they could.

Suddenly some men leaped out to meet the Mexicans,

and the two groups merged. One of the women screamed as a man caught hold of her and held her by her long hair. Two other men flung an old man to the ground and began to punch him with their fists.

Everyone was yelling and shrieking. "Salvador! Salvador!" cried Lupita, still running forward.

Then she saw that her brother was no longer running. He was struggling with a big fair-haired *gringo*. Salvador was in trouble! Sprinting toward him, Lupita reached into her sack and took out the water bottle. When she reached the two of them, Lupita hit the *gringo* on the side of his head with the bottle as hard as she could. The bottle smashed, and as it did Salvador's attacker fell to the dry, stone-covered ground.

"Help me! Help me!" The shrill wail of a girl rose above all the other noises.

Lupita stood transfixed, but Salvador jumped over the fallen *gringo* and ran to the young woman's side. He hurled himself at the man who had thrown her down. Brave Salvador! The force of his rush sent the *gringo* sprawing, and, shouting and cursing in English, he rolled down the steep hillside. Salvador grabbed the girl's outstretched hand and jerked her to her feet.

As the young woman got up, shrieking in terror, Lupita saw Tomás come back up the hill, pumping his arms to run faster. He lumbered past her and dove into some tall shrubbery. He had deserted his people, leaving them to the mercy of these lurking *gringo* bandits.

Salvador and the young woman clustered together with the rest of Tomás's party, all save the old man who lay on the hillside a distance away. Two of the men and Salvador picked up rocks and waited for the four *gringo* robbers, who walked toward them. Lupita ran to join the group. Terrified, they watched their attackers gather and stand staring at them out of greedy eyes.

All at once a spurt of dust sprang up not far from one of the *gringos*, followed by a whining sound. A rifle shot, it had come from the helicopter. The *gringos* sprang into action, leaping down the hill into the cover of trees at the bottom.

Lupita covered her face with her hands. Would the men in the helicopter shoot the rest of them now?

"*No corres*. Do not run," a voice thundered from the sky. "*Vayense para atras!* Go back."

As they started toward the border, the white beam from the helicopter held them in its light. Lupita looked back at the old man on the ground. His gray hair was splattered with blood. One of the others bent over him and then shook his head. The old man was dead.

Ay de mí! Lupita mourned for him as the young woman babbled to Salvador, "*Gracias, gracias*, thank you for what you did for me."

As the *gringo* border patrol surrounded them and took the men into custody, the woman began to sob uncontrollably. Afraid, Lupita wondered what would happen to her and Salvador.

A flashlight shone on her face, and she froze. Stifling a wail, she watched as a patrolman took Salvador by the shoulder and led him over to the group of men bound for jail.

But an instant later another *gringo* asked Salvador his age. "Fifteen, *señor*." The man shoved him back toward the women.

"What papers do you have?" a big patrolman asked.

67

The women gave up the forged papers they had gotten from Tomás while Salvador and Lupita shook their heads dumbly. Suddenly the *gringo* reached out and jerked off Lupita's baseball cap. Her long braids fell down and began to blow in the night wind.

"Another girl, eh? Three women and a boy. All right, we'll take you all back to the border and let you go."

Let them go! They would not go to jail then? "*Gracias, gracias, señores,*" Lupita burst out.

"We don't put women and children in jail. But don't try to come over here again. Remember what happened to you this time. Be glad you are alive!"

As they walked away escorted by border patrolmen, Lupita overheard an older woman complain. "*Ay de mí!* That fat coyote will not give my money back. He ran away and left us. He saved his fat hide, but my husband must go to jail. What shall I do now? I have no more money to pay another coyote."

Lupita began to tremble. What would she and Salvador do? They had gotten over the border, but only for minutes and those few minutes could easily have cost them their lives. How right Salvador had been when he said there could be robbers on both sides!

As Lupita walked along, her footsteps guided by the flashlights of the officers on her left and right, Salvador whispered, "I was proud of you down there, Lupita."

"I was proud of you, too, Salvador. But we must get a new bottle for our water."

"*Sí*, we must find a way to cross over another time."

Another time! Lupita let out a deep sigh. What difference did it make if all these people heard her? They knew she wasn't a boy. She glanced at her brother. Someday, when they returned to Ensenada, she would tell everyone what a very brave thing he had done tonight. Then perhaps he would tell them what she, small, skinny Lupita, had done too.

6

Numbly the Torres children went back to the park, where they finished the night in exhausted slumber. The next morning Lupita gave Salvador their remaining pesos. "It costs much to stay here," he said. "Even in the park we must buy food. Our money will soon be gone."

"Sí," Lupita answered with a sigh. "Salvador, I have been thinking. I have seen children beg here. I will ask the *gringas*, the women tourists, to give me money."

"No!" The word came like a clap of thunder.

"All right, I will not ask them."

But Lupita was rebellious and decided to go ahead anyway. What else could they do? If she got money from tourists, she would claim that she had found it in the park or on the sidewalks.

That very same day, following Salvador about Tijuana, Lupita approached a middle-aged *gringa* and held out her hand. As the woman passed her, she dropped a silver-colored coin into Lupita's palm. Lupita stared at her hand. Money!

To her horror, Salvador turned around just at that moment. He realized in an instant what she had done. Grabbing her by the arm, he dragged her back to the park and cuffed her. Then he pried open her fist, got hold of the coin, and threw it into the bushes. Without a word, he stalked off.

Lupita crawled through the shrubbery until she found the money. Then she sat down on a bench to await Salvador's return. She tried not to weep and betray the fact that she was a girl.

Salvador did not come back till dusk. He sat down beside her and said grimly, "It may take some time for me to find a new way to get over there, so I'm going to find work here in Tijuana if I can."

Lupita's eyes went to the idle men sitting all about them. She knew that they, too, were looking for work. Each morning they went out, but each dusk they were back in the park complaining of no work to be found and talking feverishly of ways to get into the United States.

"Perhaps I could get some shoe polish, a rag, and a brush, and then I could shine the shoes of *gringos*," Lupita said.

"No, I have seen many boys do that here. Most do not find customers. You would not make enough money to earn back the cost of the polish and the brush. No, I'll look for work, and you stay here in the park."

"Let me go with you, Salvador."

Salvador gave her a sour look. "I do not want you with me. I can walk farther and faster than you. You stay here in the park, speak to no one, and wait for me. Always be here when I return."

71

Lupita's thoughts went to Dorotea's knife, and she shivered. "Salvador, do not get into any trouble here."

"Don't worry," he mumbled. "I'll always come back to you. Now let's eat something. I'm hungry."

"Sí, Salvador."

A week went by and in that time Salvador found only a few hours' work, guarding an automobile while its owner ate in a café.

Obedient to his wishes, Lupita kept to the park. As she sat on the bench she had claimed by now as theirs, she spoke to no one. Her thoughts were of Mamá and Aunt Consuelo. *Ay de mí!* By this time both of them must think she and Salvador were over the border and in the United States.

Aunt Consuelo would be looking for them in Indio, wondering what had delayed them. Mamá would be surprised that she had not received any money from them. She would be wondering where they were, how they were faring, what kind of work they had found.

And here she sat day after day on a Tijuana park bench, waiting for Salvador to come and share another poor meal with her. Each time he returned with more crackers and beans, he told her how little money there was left.

How hard life was here in Tijuana! The eyes of some of the men in the park followed Lupita's hand each time it carried food to her mouth. *Ay de mí!* Before long she and Salvador would sit here like the hungry men and watch others eat.

Every evening Lupita scanned Salvador's face for good news. His expression began to change; his young face took on the sad look of the older men around him. He was growing thinner too, and Papá's coat hung more loosely on him. To save money both of them were eating less. Someday soon they would not eat at all!

On that dreaded day, Lupita told herself, she would go out of the park and beg. Let Salvador hit her if he wanted to. This time she would position herself beside a café on the Avenida Revolución and hold out her hand for money. In the meantime, she prayed that that day would never come.

On a chill, rainy morning, after their breakfast of crackers and water, Lupita asked, "Where do you go now, Salvador? Where will you look for work today? Will you watch *gringo* cars again?" She tried to hold him a moment longer. The day in the park was so long and lonely for her.

"I am going to the market first. Yesterday I heard a man say that overripe fruit and vegetables are given away in the market here. Perhaps I can get something for us."

Food? Given away? No, she didn't want to wait. "May I come to the market with you?"

Salvador hunched his shoulders. "I don't care. Come if you want to. Maybe you'll get more because you're so skinny."

The two of them walked side by side through the noisy town to the open-air market. There vendors sold cheeses and tortillas and cooked pork. At first the smell of the meat made Lupita's mouth water; then it made her feel sick to her stomach. No one offered them any cheese or roast pork, but they soon found that the rumor Salvador had heard was correct. An old woman selling vegetables gazed at them as they stood before her stall, and she

73

handed each of them two bruised tomatoes. How wonderful those tomatoes tasted after days of crackers and refried beans!

"*Gracias, gracias,*" Lupita told the woman, before Salvador took her by the elbow to haul her through the rest of the market.

There was no more food to be had, but just as they were about to turn around and retrace their steps, someone shouted, "*Hola*, Salvador Torres! *Hola*, Salvador!"

Who could it be? Bewildered, Salvador stopped, whirled around, and stood waiting as a gangling youth came shouldering his way through the market crowd toward them.

"Bartolo! *Hola*, Bartolo!" Salvador smiled for the first time in days. "Lupita, it is Bartolo from Ensenada. I heard he came here to Tijuana. I went to school with him."

Someone from Ensenada that she did not know? How would Salvador explain who she was? Would he tell Bartolo she was a boy?

The two youths embraced. Then Salvador pointed to her and said, "You don't know him, but this is my brother, Eduardo."

Bartolo, who had a thin moustache, laughed. "Skinny, isn't he? What brings the two of you here to Tijuana? This is no place for fishermen." He cocked his head. "You want to get over there, eh?"

"*Sí*," replied Salvador.

Bartolo said nothing more about the United States. Instead he asked, "What is the news from Ensenada? I've been gone two years now, working up here for my grandfather."

Salvador turned to Lupita. "Go back to the park. I'll tell Bartolo why we are here."

"Sí, Salvador."

They were going to talk the talk of young men, and even in the role of Eduardo there was no place for her. Glad to be free, Lupita left the market. Let Salvador be the one to tell their unhappy story to Bartolo. If Bartolo had a job, he might find work for Salvador in the market or at least give him some food. As she walked through the rain, Lupita felt her hopes rising.

It was full dark by the time Salvador came back to the park. Lupita had already lain down on the bench, which was damp from the day's rain. She shivered as she held her brother's jacket close about her.

Salvador bent down and whispered. "The sky is clearing, Lupita. When the moon rises, we will leave here."

She sat up. "Have you found work? Have you found a place for us to live? Did Bartolo do this for you?"

"No, we are going over there tonight."

"Over there?" Lupita gasped. "Salvador, is it a safe way?" Her heart started to beat more swiftly.

"I hope it will be. Ah, that Bartolo!" Salvador laughed sharply as he sat down beside her. "That Bartolo is a queer one. He hasn't changed at all. When we leave, you must do *everything* I tell you to do and you must do it quickly."

"Sí, I will. I promise," Lupita whispered. She clutched her silver cross. "Is Bartolo a coyote?"

"No, but he wants something. Everyone here wants something!"

"But our money is almost gone."

"Sí, except for a few centavos, it is. Now be quiet. Try to sleep if you can."

Sleep? How could she sleep? They were going over there again in a few hours, and Salvador thought she should sleep! What would this attempt be like? Would it be as dangerous as the last one? What would Bartolo ask of them?

When the half-moon rose over the tops of the trees, Salvador touched Lupita's arm and said, "Come. We go now."

Lupita uncurled her legs and sat up. "Where are we going?"

"To the market," he whispered.

"At night? There will be no one there, Salvador."

"Bartolo will be there. Come on."

"Sí, I come." Lupita got up and followed her brother out of the park. Looking back to their bench, she saw that it had a new tenant, a man who had lain on the sodden grass.

The part of the market where the vendors' stalls were so busy by day was dark and empty at night. But another part was filled with trucks coming and going and workers shouting at one another.

Salvador threaded his way among the trucks with Lupita following him until they found Bartolo smoking at the rear of a large green truck with board sides. This time he didn't hail Salvador, but only raised his hand in greeting.

"Come," Salvador ordered Lupita.

The three of them went behind the truck, where Bartolo spoke swiftly. "Everything is ready. The truck is loaded. Give me what you promised now."

"Sí."

Salvador reached behind his belt, took out Dorotea's knife, and gave it to Bartolo. Then he looked down at

Lupita and said in a harsh voice, "Give him your cross. Hurry."

Papá's cross! So this was Bartolo's price! Their dearest things, things they had never once considered selling to buy food. Lupita swallowed hard as her fingers closed protectively around the cross. But Salvador had given up his knife. She must give up Papá's cross also. Quickly she lifted the silver chain over her head, kissed the cross, and put it into Bartolo's open hand.

An instant later Salvador and Bartolo lifted her into the truck. It was filled with big crates constructed out of slats. She could see they were filled with vegetables.

The boys clambered onto the truck. "*Pronto*, quickly!" Bartolo caught hold of the top of a half-filled crate and lifted up the top. Inside were small, green, round things—Brussels sprouts. He scooped out a hollow place, then said to Lupita, "Get in there and lie down on your stomach. Turn your head to the side so you can breathe."

Lupita took one look at Salvador's face and decided not to protest. She stretched out on the queer-smelling vegetables, and Bartolo and Salvador covered her with them. Then Bartolo put the crate's top back on. Looking through the slats, Lupita saw Salvador lie down in the crate next to her, the one nearest the tailgate of the truck. Though she didn't know the names of the vegetables she lay among, she recognized his as onions. She watched Bartolo put the lid down on Salvador's crate and heard him whisper, "Good luck. Be quiet."

Bartolo reached up and pulled a canvas curtain across the cargo, leaving Lupita and Salvador in darkness. She heard him jump off the truck and secure the tailgate.

Panic swept over her and tears came to her eyes. In

a very small voice she called to Salvador, "I'm afraid. How do we get out of these crates?"

"The tops are not nailed down. Be quiet. Don't speak again till I call you. Pray if you want to."

Lupita prayed. She prayed to every saint she knew while she listened to men speaking in English and Spanish. Then the door slammed shut, and the truck started with a lurch. Crates began to slide over the wooden floor.

They rode for a while and then stopped for a few minutes. Lupita prayed, counting the numbers of Hail Marys she said. Lying among the Brussels sprouts, she listened to men talk about tomatoes, onions, and peppers. Then the truck started up once more. This time it drove on smoothly at high speed. Such speed frightened her. Automobiles! How she disliked them by now. She had never thought she would have so much to do with automobiles.

Lupita had no idea how far the produce truck had traveled when it came to a stop again. The driver's door opened, and a man spoke to someone in English.

"Lupita! Lupita!" came Salvador's soft cry. "Push up the top of your crate. Get out! Hurry!"

Humping her back, Lupita shoved the top of her crate up high enough so she could roll over and climb out. Vegetables scattered all over the truck bed.

Salvador was out of his crate too, standing among rolling onions. He peered out along the side of the canvas curtain, pulled it back, and then vaulted over the tailgate.

"Hurry! Come on!" he called, holding up his hands.

Lupita threw a leg over the tailgate and slid down into his arms, clutching the cloth sack to her chest. There were still some broken crackers inside.

A blaze of light illuminated the service station where the truck driver had stopped. Lupita glanced at the overhead sign; it was not in Spanish.

"Come on. Run." Salvador's hand grabbed hers and jerked her suddenly forward. Using the parked truck as cover, they ran across the road, dodging an oncoming car whose horn blared at them. They heard men's shouts behind them, but there were no sounds of pursuit.

At the edge of the highway the ground sloped sharply. Lupita and Salvador scrambled down it, through weeds still wet from the rain. They crossed a small, soggy-bottomed ditch before they got to the line of low, dark buildings on the left side of the highway.

Still hand in hand, the two of them ran until they came to a building with a projecting loading platform. Salvador halted and let go of Lupita's hand. Dropping onto all fours, he hastily crawled under the platform. Lupita followed as swiftly as she could and sat far back in the darkness.

"*Bueno*, Lupita," he panted, "you did well just now."

Breathless from the run, Lupita could only nod in the blackness. While she pressed her hand against a painful stitch in her side, she heard a booming sound in the distance. A train. She had seen trains in Tijuana.

"Lupita, did you hear that?"

"*Sí*, it is a train."

"Bartolo told me there would be trains near the warehouses just over the border. We'll go in a moment to look for the train tracks."

"Why do we want the tracks?"

"To find a train to Indio, *estupida*. Bartolo warned me not to walk along the roads near the border. He said the

79

gringo border patrol travels back and forth all the time looking for Mexicans, asking for cards to show that they are *pochos*, Mexican-Americans, or that they have a card that says they can work here. They will catch us when we do not understand their English."

Lupita said nothing, but she felt a little better about having given Bartolo her cross. This Bartolo knew a thing or two.

"Bartolo told me we are to stay hidden and to listen hard," Salvador continued.

"Listen?"

"*Sí*, listen."

Huddled under the loading dock, Lupita heard nothing but the small night wind and the noise of the wet weeds brushing against one another. Then all at once she heard voices whispering in Spanish.

"That is what Bartolo said we were to listen for—someone speaking Spanish," Salvador said. "Come out now, Lupita. Bartolo said not to travel alone. It is not safe."

They crawled out and stood in the shadows beside the warehouse. Soon a little group of Mexicans, a man, a woman, and two half-grown children, came past them.

"Call out to them, Lupita," Salvador ordered. "Ask about Indio."

"*Señor, señora*," Lupita called softly. "*Por favor, señor.*"

"Who is it?" The man's voice sounded startled.

"My brother Salvador Torres and me. We want to find the city of Indio. Where is it, do you know?"

"No." The man hesitated, then said, "Come here. Let me see you."

Lupita and Salvador stepped out of the shadows. They saw a small, overall-clad man with a wispy beard.

"I am named Rosario," he said. "Do you have cards to work here?"

"No, Señor Rosario," replied Salvador.

"Ah." He sighed. "Then you are like me. I have come over here four times, but always the *gringos* caught me and sent me back. I have brought my wife and children with me this time. We are going to Los Angeles."

"It was lonely for him in Los Angeles without us," Rosario's wife explained.

Salvador interrupted, "Do you know how I can find out where Indio is?"

"No." Señor Rosario shook his head. "But this Indio must be north of here. Everything in California is north of here. We will take a northbound train ourselves. Come with us."

"How do we know where to get off the train?" Salvador asked.

"I will tell you when we come to Los Angeles. I will look after you two until we get there."

"*Gracias, señor,*" said Salvador.

Bueno, some good luck at last, thought Lupita, as she brought up the rear of the little procession.

Señor Rosario soon found the railroad tracks, and they all started walking northward. How fortunate they were to fall in with this clever Señor Rosario. In a while the man lifted his hand and pointed to some buildings beside the tracks. They walked over and then halted in the shadows, waiting.

They did not wait long before a round yellow light came toward them. Then they heard the sound of a train. It passed them slowly, grinding to a halt ahead of where they stood. Lupita saw scarlet sparks rise from the metal

81

wheels as they slowed to a stop. Quickly men with flash-lights came down off the train, and more came out of some buildings over the tracks.

The men set to work uncoupling freight cars and at-taching new ones onto the train.

Señor Rosario spoke above the noise. "We go as soon as the men with the lights have left."

Finally the railroad workers finished. Señor Rosario went forward with his family trailing him. Lupita and Salvador came behind. Rosario stopped beside a boxcar with a half-open door. He lifted one child into the car after the other. Then he got in himself and helped his wife scramble up.

Lupita was about to pull herself up too, when Salvador caught her by the arm and pointed to the next car. It was a strangely shaped metal one with a tower on top.

"It carries flour or grain," Salvador whispered rapidly into her ear. "Rosario says it will be empty when it goes north to Los Angeles. He has ridden in such cars before. He would choose it now, but his children are too small to get out of it. Come on. Hurry."

There was a steel ladder on the side of the hopper car. Salvador pulled himself up, lifted up the metal cover, and dropped down inside. Lupita followed, going up the ladder as fast as she could and falling with a thud onto the bottom of the car.

Never had she known such absolute darkness. "Sal-vador!" she called out, frightened.

"I am here. Be quiet. Do you have the cloth bag and the matches?"

"Sí, I have them."

"Get me a match."

Lupita reached into the bag and after some rummaging found the matches. Salvador struck one along the side of the steel car, and during its brief blaze they inspected the hopper. To Lupita's surprise, it was not black at all, but dusty white. There was a ladder up to the top on the inside too.

Suddenly Lupita heard shouts. She sank down as Salvador blew out the match. "What is it?" she asked fearfully.

"I do not know. I'll go up to see."

Panic-stricken, Lupita was not about to be left alone in the darkness. She climbed up behind Salvador and stuck her head up over the turret. Holding fast to Salvador, she crowded her slight body against his.

Ay de mí!

Men with flashlights and pistols on their hips were walking beside the train. When they came to a boxcar, they hauled open the doors and shone the lights inside. A man with a bass voice called out in Spanish, "*Traigo una pistola. Levantense los manos*! I have a pistol. Raise your hands."

Lupita looked on in dismay as Señor Rosario and his family jumped out of their boxcar. To her surprise, three young Mexican men followed them. The railroad guards handcuffed Señor Rosario to one of the young men and handcuffed the other two together. Another guard led Señor Rosario's weeping wife and children away. Tears came to Lupita's eyes.

"Lupita, get your head down," Salvador hissed, as he ducked his head out of sight below the turret. Lupita scrunched down, and Salvador quickly pulled the hatch shut as far as he could. Seconds later they saw the beam of a flashlight through the crack that remained open. Lupita held her breath in terror. Would they be flushed out too? Would one of the railroad guards climb up to the hopper car, open the turret, and shine his light down inside the car?

7

Salvador caught hold of Lupita and carried her halfway down the ladder, where they stopped and hung, motionless. "*Silencio*," he whispered into her ear.

Lupita stopped breathing. When a loud clanging sound announced the presence of one of the guards outside their metal car, she gasped in spite of herself.

To her great relief, no one came to inspect the car. Finally she heard the voices of the *gringo* guards fade, and then Salvador said, "We can go down now, Lupita."

They dropped and Lupita sank in exhaustion. In a few minutes, the freight train gave a sudden lurching that flung her backward. Just as she got to her feet in the dark, a second lurch threw her over again. At last the train started up in earnest, going slowly at first, then picking up speed.

"Salvador!" Lupita cried softly, afraid to get up.

"I am here. Don't be afraid." He laughed triumphantly.

Lupita understood why he was happy. They were in the United States at last and on their way to Indio and Aunt

Consuelo and jobs! Unlike poor Señor Rosario and his family, she and Salvador had succeeded. Lupita put out her hand and touched Salvador's arm for reassurance.

On and on the train went, making *click-clack* noises on the rails, grinding metal on metal, until it came to a stop. Lupita had no idea how long they had been in the hopper, but it must have been an hour at least.

She and Salvador did not move. They sat together in the darkness as their car was uncoupled, put onto a siding, and with a good deal of jerking and jolting coupled to another train. All this work was done to the loud accompaniment of *gringo* voices outside.

"Where are we, Salvador?" Lupita asked.

"I do not know. Perhaps in this Los Angeles Señor Rosario talked about." Then he added, "Lupita, I think we are being attached to another train. Perhaps that will take us to Indio."

"Sí, to Indio," Lupita agreed happily.

The train rolled smoothly to the east, clattering over the rails, booming warnings at automobile crossings like some great bull. After a long time, it stopped.

Their car was one of three taken off. Uncoupled, it glided noiselessly along the rails until it was brought to a halt with a terrific thump. A moment later the second uncoupled car from the freight struck it, knocking Lupita and Salvador over on their backs.

Next they heard the sounds of the freight train's engine as it pulled out of the yards, leaving them behind. They sat in the bottom of the hopper, listening to the train's noises fade away. All about them was silence, an eerie, dead silence.

Where were they? Had they come to Indio?

"We'll wait awhile in here," Salvador told Lupita. "Then I'll go up to the top and look around."

Lupita could hear her brother's labored, quick breathing. He was as nervous as she was. After five minutes, he got up and started to search for the ladder. A soft grunt signaled that he found it.

In a minute, he was back, stumbling into her. "Lupita, there's nothing here but tracks and buildings and three railroad cars. There are no guards. Nobody. Dawn's coming. I've seen a better place for us to hide. Hurry up."

Delighted to be out of the hopper's blackness, Lupita followed him up the ladder, through the turret, and down the exterior steps to the ground. Streaks of pink and gold were showing in the east.

"Come on, Lupita."

They went along to the car behind them. It was a boxcar like the one Señor Rosario and his family had entered. Suddenly Lupita held back.

Salvador grabbed her hand and spoke softly. "It will be cooler in here when the sun is up, Lupita. We can see outside, and we don't have to worry that anyone will fill it with flour or grain."

Lupita glanced back over her shoulder at the hopper car with horror! *Ay de mí*, she had not thought of that. Of course, the hopper must have been brought here to be filled with something. She shivered, thinking of suffocating under so much flour, and scrambled up into the boxcar as fast as she could.

Thirsty and still hungry after devouring what little food remained, the two of them sat in one corner of the boxcar until sunset. They had seen no one yet and had decided to go out after dark to find out where they were.

Dusk had fallen when they suddenly heard a dog barking. The two of them froze in their corner. A dog? It went on barking, but over it came a baritone voice singing:

"In the graveyard of forgetfulness
Give burial to my longing,
Deny that I have loved you,
I ask you as a favor.
Te lo pido, por favor."

As the man repeated the last line, Lupita realized that she knew the song. The singer must be Mexican or a *pocho!*

"Salvador," whispered Lupita eagerly.

"Call out to him, Lupita. He will think you are a boy and don't mean him any harm."

Lupita went to the side of the door of the boxcar and called, "*Señor, señor, por favor?*"

"Who is there?" asked the man in Spanish.

Lupita remembered the name Salvador had bestowed upon her in Tijuana. "Eduardo Torres. *Señor, señor,* where am I?"

The man asked a strange question. "Who is with you?"

"My brother, Salvador." She hesitated, then asked, "Are you *mexicano?*"

"No, I am *americano.*"

"He is a *pocho,*" Lupita hissed to Salvador.

"Come down out of there. I work for this railroad. You are not supposed to be in there. This car is railroad property."

Ay de mí, a guard! Were *pochos* railroad guards, too?

"*Guardia?*" she cried.

The man laughed and called up to her, "Come down. No, I am not the guard. Let me have a look at you."

Lupita peeked carefully around the corner of the boxcar door into the brown eyes of a stocky man wearing blue coveralls and a high-crowned blue cap. He was smiling while he patted a large brown dog, who was not even growling now. A quick glance showed Lupita that he had a flashlight but no pistol.

"Where are we, *señor*?" she repeated.

"In Colton. Where do you want to be?"

"Indio, where our Aunt Consuelo lives."

"Indio? That is eighty *gringo* miles from here over the San Gorgonio Mountains and into the desert." He shook his head. "Come down now, *muchachos*."

"*Sí*," replied Lupita, crestfallen that they were so far from their destination, but relieved by the friendliness of this *pocho*.

After she and Salvador had got down, the man asked them, "Did you just come up from Mexico?" He chuckled. "No, don't tell me. I don't want to hear you lie. I know that you did."

"*Sí*, we did," agreed Salvador, eyeing the dog. It had begun growling. "How do we get to this Indio then, *señor*?"

The man smiled. "You could take a bus from Colton to Indio if you have the money. It would cost you around three *gringo* dollars each."

"We have only pesos," Salvador said. They didn't have the equivalent of six *gringo* dollars in any event.

"Pesos are no good here." The man spoke very pleasantly. "But even if you could take the bus you don't know enough English to buy the tickets or to ask someone where to get off when you come to Indio. Surely *la migra* would catch you."

"*La migra?*" Lupita asked.

"*Sí*, the *gringo* immigration officers. They hunt all the time for people like you. They look for aliens who do not have green-card permits to work over here."

"They are not the border police then?" Salvador asked.

"No. They work everywhere, not only at the border."

La migra? Lupita filed the name in her memory. First Mexican robbers, then the fat coyote, then *gringo* robbers on the hillside, the Border Patrol, the railroad guards, and now *la migra!*

She looked at Salvador, and he looked at her. "*Señor, por favor,*" he asked, "tell us what road to take to Indio. We will walk there."

"Will you? The men of *la migra* travel that road all the time in their automobiles." He grinned at Lupita. "My name is Esposito, Hector Esposito. Perhaps I can find a safer way for you to get to Indio later on. You two came here to work, eh?"

"*Sí, señor*, we did," answered Salvador.

Esposito nodded. "My brother owns a café here that serves Mexican food. He sometimes needs older boys to work for him. Beside the café, there is a little motel that needs workers too. It is a pity that your brother isn't a girl. . . ."

"Señor Esposito." Lupita took off the baseball cap and let her braids fall down her back. "I am Lupita Torres, not Eduardo," she said shyly. "We come from Ensenada. I have worked there as a maid in a hotel, helping my mother."

"*Bueno.* Go to my car, the blue van over there." He pointed to the west of the tracks. "Get into the back and stay there until I finish my work here. Then I will take you to my brother's café. Are you hungry?"

At Lupita's nod he said, "There are tortillas in a metal box in my car. Eat a tortilla, but leave the other food for me. There is coffee, too, in a jug. Have some coffee if you wish."

"*Gracias*, Señor Esposito," Salvador said, as he and Lupita started toward the van.

Minutes later they were sitting inside the old blue van, eating corn tortillas and drinking coffee from the thermos. After she had eaten, Lupita immediately fell asleep on the van's floor, and a little later Salvador nodded off too.

They were awakened several hours later when Señor Esposito and his dog climbed into the front seat. They drove through the town of Colton to an alley behind a café and motel. There Esposito opened the van's rear, ordered the children out, and led them into the café kitchen through the back door. "Rodrigo, Rodrigo," he called out.

While they waited, Lupita looked about, sniffing the familiar odors of chili and peppers. The big kitchen was divided into several parts. Three cooks in white clothing worked at the big stoves, putting beans, rice, and enchiladas onto plates that dark-haired waitresses in bright-red dresses picked up at a counter. They spoke to each other in Spanish. On the other side of the kitchen stood a black-haired boy about Salvador's age, scraping uneaten food off plates into big garbage pails. Then he put the soiled dishes into a square metal machine and pulled a lever, which brought hot water and hot air through the device. As Lupita looked on in wonder, dishes rapidly came out clean and dry.

A short man in a ruffled white shirt, black string tie,

red sash, and black trousers came out finally to look at Lupita and Salvador. Then he asked Hector in Spanish, "Where did you find these two?"

"In the customary place, Rodrigo, the freight yard. They seek work."

"Do they? They always seek jobs." Rodrigo Esposito had a queer, rumbling chuckle that started deep in his barrel chest. "How old are they?"

Salvador raised their ages. "Twenty, *señor*, and my sister is seventeen."

The café owner chuckled once more. "I would say fifteen and twelve, but no matter. I need some help here. Do you speak any English?"

"No, they don't, Rodrigo," Hector Esposito replied. "They are called Salvador and Lupita Torres. The girl says she has worked as a chambermaid in Mexico."

"*Bueno*. Perhaps the motel can use her. This boy can work in here with the dishwashing machine. Have you told him yet what he must pay?"

Pay? Lupita felt stabbed. Whom did they have to pay?

"No, I have not told them." Hector laughed. "You tell them. Your Spanish is as good as mine, brother. Just be sure to pay me my share. *Adiós*, Rodrigo." Without another word, the *pocho* turned and left.

The café owner motioned to Salvador and Lupita. "Come into my office."

Lupita and Salvador followed him in to a small room behind the kitchen where he sat down at a desk and looked at them. "In order for you to work here, you and your sister must have what is called a social-security card. I can get one for you from someone who forges them. Of course, this card costs money. Salvador, I will pay you two dollars and fifty cents an hour. That is about fifty pesos."

Lupita gasped at the amount. Salvador was very lucky.

The man smiled and went on. "The first week you work for me you will pay one third of what you earn to the man who makes your forged card. You will pay another third to my brother, Hector."

"A third to him? Salvador asked in astonishment.

"*Sí*. Would you have got work without Hector? He surely saved you from *la migra*. You and your sister can eat your meals here and rent a room from me in a house I own behind the motel. You will only have to pay one hundred and forty dollars a month. That is very cheap here in the United States. Now, boy, you can get something to eat while I take your sister to my cousin, Señor Elfren, who owns the motel. When you have finished, tell Valentin, the boy at the dishwasher, to show you how to run the machine." Señor Rodrigo waved his hand and Salvador went out to the kitchen.

"*Muchacha*, you come with me."

Señor Elfren Esposito was small boned, thin, and older than his cousin. The two men spoke in Spanish while Lupita stood by, gazing past them at the lobby filled with with beautiful, red-vinyl-covered chairs and tile-top, black iron tables.

Suddenly Señor Elfren asked her, "Where did you work in Mexico?"

"In Ensenada, *señor*, at the hotel of Señor Aguilar where my mother works. I helped her clean and make beds for *gringo* tourists."

"So?" Señor Elfren addressed the café owner. "I guess I have a uniform small enough for this girl." He turned to Lupita. "One thing, *muchacha*. Do not expect to enjoy an afternoon siesta here as you do in Mexico. We work all day until six o'clock." He spoke to Señor Rodrigo again. "I'll pay two dollars and twenty-five cents an hour and put Concha in charge of her."

"My mother taught me the words *sheet* and *towel* and *soap, señor*," Lupita volunteered.

"*Sí*," he replied disinterestedly. Then he asked the café owner, "Has she been told of the forged card?"

"She heard me tell her brother. She knows she is to pay Hector and her rent."

"*Bueno*. She can start work tomorrow morning." Señor Elfren sniffed. "She's thin as a snake. Can you fatten her up so she'll be strong enough to run a vacuum cleaner, Rodrigo?"

"I'll try. Her brother is stuffing himself right now. Come on, girl, you're next to eat."

Señor Rodrigo showed Lupita the small, yellow-painted house on the other side of the alley. "That is where you will stay with your brother and Concha, one of the maids from the hotel. The other boy who operates my dishwasher lives there too. They are both Mexicans like yourself. When you and your brother are not working, try to stay inside the house unless you're with people who know some English. Do not call attention to yourself here."

"*Sí*, Señor Esposito, *gracias, gracias*." Her heart singing with joy, Lupita said, "I'm not hungry, so I'll go to the house if you don't mind."

"Suit yourself." Esposito turned toward the café.

Lupita, alone at last, opened the door of the little house where she and Salvador were to live. They had work!

The first week would go by fast, and when they had paid Señor Hector and the man who would forge the social-security cards and Señor Rodrigo for their beds, they would still have something to send to Mamá. The week after there would be even more money. If she and Salvador were to stay inside the house, how could they spend their money? How quickly their luck had changed from bad to good!

The yellow house was sparsely furnished, but to Lupita it seemed very fine. Each of the two bedrooms contained two single beds, a chair, a chest of drawers, and a clothes closet. There was a tiny bathroom and a little living room, too, with four chairs, a table with a plastic cloth, and a transistor radio. The beautiful draperies were of paper, printed with big, red poinsettia blossoms.

Concha, a thin woman, older than Mamá, was friendly and full of advice. She told Lupita at once, "You have just come to this country and know nothing as yet. I have a warning for you. Sometimes the *gringos* who stay in the motel try to talk with the maids. If one does speak to you, smile and get away as fast as you can. Point to a room down the hall to make him think you are too busy to talk. Do not let him know you are from Mexico and cannot speak English, or he may call *la migra* to come get you."

"Why would a *gringo* tell *la migra* about me?"

Concha laughed. "Ah, who knows what a *gringo* will do? They are very strange. Work hard and do not talk to anyone, not even to me. Señor Elfren does not like his maids to stand around talking to one another."

"Sí." Lupita nodded. Señor Aguilar had not liked that either. She looked across the living room at Salvador, who was talking with Valentin. They must be talking about the dishwasher. Valentin was making motions with his hands as if he was using machinery.

Lupita looked away from them to the poinsettias on the draperies as she relaxed in her chair. *Bueno!* Concha would teach her, and Valentin would help Salvador. How lucky they were to find work so soon and friendly Mexicans to help them.

The next morning, after a stand-up breakfast in the café, Lupita started her job as a chambermaid. The work was similar to what Mamá did in Ensenada, but Lupita found it very hard. There she had helped out now and then, but now she had fifteen bedrooms on the second floor of the motel to clean by herself! Floors to vacuum, bathrooms to scour, furniture to dust, and twenty-five beds to change. Sixteen were single beds, but the other nine were very large, so large that Lupita had to keep circling them and lifting the great mattresses to tuck in the sheets and blankets. By midday her arms ached, and she could hardly push the vacuum over the thick rugs. After that heavy work, cleaning the toilets and putting up fresh towels seemed restful.

Halfway through the afternoon, Señor Elfren came up the outside stairs to check Lupita's work. He asked her what rooms she had finished, and then he unlocked their doors and went inside. She waited, worried, on the veranda overlooking the street. Would her work be good enough? Was she too weak to suit him?

When he came out of the last room, he nodded at her and went down the steps to the lobby. He was satisfied. Lupita let out her breath and went back to work.

By six o'clock she was exhausted, almost too weary to talk with Salvador, who came to sit beside her in Señor Rodrigo's kitchen and eat a dinner of enchiladas, beans, and rice.

"How did it go? Did you have any trouble?" he asked.

"No, but it is hard. Some of the beds are very big."

"Sí, the work here is hard." Salvador mopped his forehead with his arm. "The water in the dishwasher is very hot. If I am not careful, I can get scalded. How much food these *gringos* leave on their plates! I wish we had had it in Tijuana." He smiled. "But I like the dishwashing machine. It is interesting."

"*Bueno*, Salvador," Lupita was too tired to say more.

"Lupita, I have talked with Valentin while we work."

Lupita's interest rose. "Señor Rodrigo does not care if you talk and work at the same time?"

"No, not as long as we get the dishes washed. Valentin has told me how to send money down to Mexico. He knows all of the ways."

Lupita finished her food, being careful not to get a stain on her white uniform. "What are they?"

"He says I can take our money to a bank here, open an account, and send Mamá a piece of paper called a 'check.' She can take it to a bank in Ensenada and get pesos for it."

Go to a *gringo* bank? Trust *yanqui* strangers! Lupita shook her head fearfully.

Salvador nodded in agreement. "Another way is to go to the post office and buy a money order to send to Mamá. One of the *pocho* cooks, the fat one over there"—Salvador jerked his thumb toward the kitchen, and Lupita saw a heavyset middle-aged man behind the counter—"is a good

97

man. He told Valentin he would get us the money orders. But that is not the way Valentin sends money to his family in Mexicali."

"How does he do it?"

"He writes a letter and puts cash into the envelope. Then he seals it, registers it at the post office, and mails it."

Lupita's eyes grew wide as she leaned over the table to speak softly. "Salvador, someone could steal the money!"

"Not if the letter is registered. Valentin's always reaches his family. They write and tell him so. Concha takes his letters and registers them. She speaks English well enough for that, he says."

Lupita's teeth sunk into her lower lip. Sí, this would be the safest way, less danger of being caught by *la migra*. After a moment she nodded. "When we are paid, I will write Mamá a letter, and we will include what money we can. I will tell her that we will send more in the next letter."

Salvador grinned as he began to eat his third tortilla. "What will you write to her?"

Lupita stared gravely at him, then looked about her at the busy, noisy kitchen. "I will not write her of the money we must pay for cards in order to work here. I will not tell her how we were robbed in Mexico or about the coyote or about the old man who was murdered. I won't tell her how hard it was for us in Tijuana. That would make her sad. I *will* tell her how we crossed over covered up with vegetables. That will make her laugh, and Uncle Antonio too. I will not tell her about giving up Papá's cross or Dorotea's knife, but I will tell her that we have good-paying jobs here and that we will go to Indio as soon as we can. I'll tell her that we will stay in Colton

98

until we have learned the English we need to take a bus, and I'll promise to write to Aunt Consuelo and tell her where we are so she won't be worried about us."

Salvador nodded approvingly. "*Bueno*, that will do. But when we are paid the first time, we must also buy some new clothing. We have only rags."

"*Sí*, I know. I need to buy a dress so I can go to Mass. Concha told me last night that there is a church here that *pochos* go to. They speak Spanish there. She said if I had a dress I could go with her. Clothing costs much here in the United States, but I will buy the cheapest dress I can find."

Salvador's look soured. He did not like the idea of buying a cheap shirt. He liked handsome things, things that had luster and color. But Lupita knew he would be careful of the price.

"Salvador, where will we buy our clothes?"

"Valentin knows a store where they speak Spanish. He will take me there. It probably sells dresses for girls, too. Get Concha to take you the day she registers our first letter to Mamá."

"*Sí*, I will ask Concha."

Lupita's first week in Colton was spent working, eating in Señor Rodrigo's café, listening to music on the little radio, and sleeping in a room with Concha. Two *gringos* in the motel tried to talk with her, but she found Concha's advice worked very well. Neither *gringo* followed her when she hurried down the hallway and into an empty room.

During that week Lupita also learned that Concha was not always so agreeable. Sometimes after work she was cross and snappish, complaining that her feet hurt. Sometimes she came back to the little house to lie down before she went over to the café to eat. At those times, Lupita left her alone; she and Salvador would need Concha's help and goodwill.

On Friday morning, Salvador and Lupita received their wages. Though what they owed for the forged cards and a week's room and board had been subtracted, there was still money left over. Enough to buy a shirt and a dress and to send some to Mamá.

That Friday morning Concha was in a better mood, and she promised she would cross the street to the post office on her afternoon break and mail Lupita's letter. At noon Lupita got the letter she had written, nervously put in the cash she and Salvador had agreed to send, sealed it, and handed it to Concha along with four dollars for the registration.

The next day, after lunch, Concha took Lupita to a discount store close to the motel and helped her pick out a dress. It was made of dark-blue cotton, had a belt, and the cloth was so heavy that Lupita did not need to buy a petticoat.

Neither Lupita nor Concha had to work on Sundays so they went to Mass at the small, white *pocho* church. There Lupita found nothing to make her uncomfortable. The priest spoke in Spanish, and she was able to light a candle at the altar for Papá's soul, as she was certain Mamá was doing this morning in Ensenada.

As they left the church, Concha asked Lupita, "Did you pray for your family?"

"*Sí*, for Mamá and my brothers and sisters."

"And for Salvador and yourself?"

"No, I forgot to do that." Lupita stopped on the church steps. "But I gave thanks for coming here safely to Colton."

"You should have prayed for yourself. Take care, Lupita. Take care not to anger Señor Elfren or Señor Rodrigo. Do not make them displeased." As they left the steps, Concha went on, "They can call *la migra* whenever they want to."

"Why would they do that, Señorita Concha?"

Concha's eyes bored into Lupita's. "Because some other Mexican might come along willing to work for less money than you or Salvador. Perhaps they will like some other girl's looks better. To get rid of you, all they have to do is call *la migra* and say they have just learned that you are not a *pocha* but a wetback."

Lupita's hand went to her mouth in terror.

"I am always afraid," Concha continued. "Day and night I am afraid. Do not be bold. Pray for yourselves and be careful."

"*Sí*, I will be careful." Then Lupita asked to change the subject, "Where did you learn the English you know?"

"From the chambermaid who was here before you. She went back to her family in Mexico."

"You did not learn it from a book then?"

"No, no." Concha looked astonished.

"Should I learn some English too?"

"A little would help you, I think. When I have time, I will teach you the words I know."

"*Gracias*. Perhaps someday I will buy a book that is in Spanish and in English, too."

"No," Concha advised. "You would have to go to a bookstore, and the person there would surely know that you are a Mexican and call *la migra*."

Again *la migra*! Always *la migra*. It must be everywhere.

Yet Lupita could not believe that anything terrible would happen in Colton. From what she had seen, the small *gringo* city was a pretty one, even if it had no blue ocean bay like Ensenada. Instead, it was ringed with sharp-peaked mountains that changed from blue to brown to violet at different times of day. The houses were constructed of wood, and they were painted white, yellow, green, and tan instead of pink, blue, and lavender like the homes in Tijuana and Ensenada. Concha had told her that only one family lived in each house. How rich these *gringos* were!

Yet there were some things that Lupita missed. No trumpet and guitar music could be heard on the streets. *Sí*, there was Latin music in Señor Rodrigo's café, but it was so soft she had to strain her ears to hear it. Concha said that was how the *gringos* like their music, almost inaudible, as if their ears were very tender. There were no people selling things on the streets either. All of the buying and selling went on indoors.

These *gringos* did not smile at one another or stop to chat. They seemed to go about their business as quickly and seriously as possible. Even eating in Señor Rodrigo's café, which should have been a great pleasure, was speedily done. *Sí*, Concha was correct in saying that *gringos* were very strange indeed!

The next week Lupita struck up an acquaintance with Linda, one of the *pocha* waitresses in the café. They often talked while Lupita was eating in the kitchen.

On Wednesday, Linda took Lupita to the shoe store next door and helped her buy a much-needed pair of white shoes with sturdy crepe soles. She later agreed with a complaining Lupita that the shoes had cost far too much money.

Lupita admired Linda's pretty face, her red fingernails, her golden hoop earrings, and the scent of perfume that always surrounded her. Clearly she was a favorite of Señor Rodrigo; he always had a smile for her even when he had none for anyone else. The *pocho* cooks told Salvador that Linda made more money in tips than any of the other waitresses because she was the most popular. As Lupita watched her admiringly, she thought that being a waitress must be a very good job. She would like to be able to do that work herself, but even in a Mexican restaurant a waitress must know English. Almost all of the customers would be *gringos*. How lucky Linda was to be a *pocha* and know English as well as Spanish!

That Friday evening Lupita was just starting to eat her supper when Linda burst suddenly into the kitchen, waving her hands in the air. She ran over to Lupita and whispered into her ear, "*La migra* is here. They have come to raid for Mexicans. Get away! Hurry!" Then she whirled about and rushed back through the swinging doors.

La migra! In the dining room on the other side of the door!

8

Lupita leaped up, ran over to the dishwasher, and pulled on Salvador's arm. "*La migra* has come! Linda says for us to get away, *pronto!*" she hissed.

Salvador stopped, dropping a dish on the floor. Then he called out softly to Valentin, who stood on the side of the machine, "*La migra!*"

But Valentin went on working. He couldn't hear over the noise. Salvador didn't wait to deliver his warning a second time. Without removing his apron, he bolted after Lupita out the back door into the alley. Passing her, he ran to a boarded-off area that concealed the café's dozen garbage cans. Quickly he dropped down among them, and Lupita squatted beside him.

In a minute, they saw Valentin come out the rear door, handcuffed to a *gringo*. They went to a car and got into the back seat. A few minutes later a weeping Concha was brought out of the motel and also put into the car. Afterward two of the three immigration officials went into the little yellow house. Señor Rodrigo followed them, shaking his head.

Lupita whispered, "Perhaps they will see that four of us are living there. Perhaps they will wait for us." She bit her knuckles in fear.

Frowning, Salvador growled, "They won't stay in the house, but they might come back to it." He paused, then whispered, "Lupita, we won't go back there." He stripped off his apron and draped it over a garbage can. "When the cars leave, we're going to start for Indio. We'll walk there."

"Tonight, Salvador?"

"Sí."

"Do you know the road to take?"

"Sí. I asked the cook last week to tell me where it is. He told me what number road goes there. *Gringo* roads have numbers like Mexican roads, and numbers look the same even if words don't. There is nobody to buy bus tickets for us, so we have to walk. But first I'll see Señor Rodrigo and ask for the last of my wages. You go ask Señor Elfren for yours."

Lupita nodded. Salvador was right. She wanted to leave as quickly as possible too.

The Torres children kept watch from their hiding place until the Immigration and Naturalization Service car drove off with its prisoners in the back seat. Señor Rodrigo came slowly back toward the kitchen, looking at the ground.

Lupita and Salvador stood up and intercepted the café owner. "It was a bad business this time," he said, shaking his head. "The man who forged the cards was caught. He told the police that some Mexican nationals were working here. The police told *la migra*, and you know the rest. You two are lucky that they didn't find you." He nodded. "Lucky that Linda warned you in time. Often

105

la migra come back again soon, so it would be best for you two to leave here now."

"It is our wish to go, *señor*," Salvador told him. "Pay me what you owe me, and we will go tonight."

Señor Rodrigo nodded. "That will be all right with me. Go to the house and get your things. Then come back to the kitchen. I have money in the cash register."

While Salvador walked across the alley to the yellow house, Lupita went to the motel. She found Señor Elfren and told him that she and Salvador were leaving right away.

The motelkeeper agreed. "*Sí*, go somewhere where nobody will know your cards are forged. I'll give you your wages as soon as you get out of my maid's uniform. That must remain here."

Ten minutes later Lupita and Salvador came out of the yellow house, wearing their old clothes. Although they looked the same as they had leaving Tijuana, this time they had money in their pockets. The thought was a comfort to Lupita.

But they must buy food for the journey; more crackers and canned beans and perhaps some cheese too. Most certainly they would need canteens for water.

Lupita touched Salvador's arm as he came out of the kitchen stuffing dollars into his pockets. "Salvador, *por favor*, do not try to get a ride for us from any automobiles here."

He laughed. "Do you think I could forget what happened the last time?" He pointed to his feet. "Now I trust these most of all. The cook wrote down the way for me while I waited for old Rodrigo. He said that *pochos* may try to help us and we should trust them. He is a good man.

106

I will miss him." Salvador paused. "I will miss Valentin, too."

Lupita nodded, thinking of Linda, who had saved them. Sí, there were good *pochos*.

As they passed behind the rear of the motel and café, Lupita sighed deeply. She had left the blue dress hanging in the closet. Salvador had told her it must remain behind. How could she pretend to be a boy if she was caught with a dress stuffed into her jacket pocket?

Hearing her sigh, Salvador said angrily, "Don't start that again! Remember, you are my brother. What did I name you in Tijuana?"

"Eduardo. I am Eduardo." Lupita stifled a second sigh. She didn't much like the name, but Eduardo she must pretend to be until they reached the fine house of Aunt Consuelo and her *pocho* husband. He would surely be a good man and find work for them. He would know the ways of the United States.

Lupita looked up at the sky for the first stars. Sí, there was one, not far from the new moon, the very one she had pointed out as Papá's star in Ensenada just last month. How long ago that seemed. Lupita's chest tightened with loneliness. The company in the little yellow house had not made up for the loss of her family.

She straightened her shoulders. "Salvador, living with Aunt Consuelo will be like living at home. I saw a photograph of Aunt Consuelo when she and Mamá were girls. They look very much alike, even if she is rich and Mamá is poor."

At an open shopping center on Valley Boulevard, they bought two canteens in a hardware store and some food in the supermarket. By now both of them were familiar with *gringo* money and how cash registers worked. It was easy to watch the figures on the cash register, then hand over paper money and pocket the change. The *gringo* clerks didn't seem to notice them, nor did the service-station boy when they filled their canteens from the water hose.

When they had what they needed they started down Valley Boulevard, traveling east. In two hours they were out of the city and in open country.

Salvador stopped. "The highway we need is called a 'freeway,' but the *gringo* law doesn't permit us to walk there."

"Why not?"

"The cook told me it is too dangerous. He said that we should travel on the city streets, keeping the freeway in sight or in hearing distance all the time."

"How can we hear it?"

"He says the freeway roars like the sea because the many cars go so swiftly on it."

Lupita frowned. Cars, more cars! "Where will we find the right road, Salvador?"

"Out in the fields here. The cook said we would come to a place where several roads come together in the sky."

"In the sky?" Lupita pressed the old cloth sack with their food to her breast. Who had ever heard of roads in the sky? Could even *gringos* build roads like that?

A half hour later, when she spied the enormous elevated interchange loom up ahead of them, she gasped and put one hand to the side of her face. There they were—the roads in the sky! The streams of white and red dots, head-lights and taillights, astounded her.

"Salvador!" she whispered. "What shall we do? What direction do we take?"

"We go up into the mountains over the San Gorgonio pass, and from there into the desert. You have seen the mountains from Colton."

"But how do we find the road we need?" She pointed to the great interchange overhead.

"Come on. The cook told me how to do it."

Lupita followed Salvador into the meadows that lay beneath the vast concrete arches. They ducked under barbed-wire fences and scrambled in and out of ditches that crisscrossed beneath the freeways, ever aware of the frightening, oceanlike roaring over their heads.

Salvador soon found the road he wanted. He pointed it out and said, "Lupita, we'll walk in the fields alongside this big road as far as we can. Then we can hide in a ditch if a car stops."

"Where will we sleep tonight?"

"We won't sleep tonight at all. We must travel by night while it is cool and dark. At dawn, I'll find a place for us to sleep."

After a few more miles, Lupita saw that the shape of the freeway had changed. It was no longer straight and flat, but had begun to dip, and now it ran at the bottom of high banks covered with green plants.

"We have to leave sight of the freeway now," Salvador told her, "and walk on the bordering streets. Not even a goat could walk along these steep banks."

Lupita agreed. What strange roads *gringos* built—sometimes up in the sky, at other times out of sight in the earth! She felt as small and frightened as she had in the hopper car, and she prayed they would get to Aunt Consuelo soon.

That first day they slept under a small bridge in the suburbs of Riverside. The bridge spanned a dry gully, which sheltered them as they slept. At nightfall, they started out once more.

After several hours they found Highway 60 and walked along parallel streets within hearing distance of it. At daybreak, Salvador found a large concrete culvert, part of a drainage system, for them to crawl into. Lupita's sleep was fitful. She kept awakening to think of the climb they would soon have to make through the mountains and of the desert that lay on the other side. Uncle Antonio told her of the deserts in Baja California, describing them as terrible places of heat, sand, and bare rocks, with no water to be found.

As she and Salvador set out that night, Lupita asked, "Have you thought about water for our canteens in the mountains and the desert?"

"*Sí*, we will find water at gas stations. The cook said there are service stations everywhere in this state."

"But *la migra* could be waiting at the stations."

Salvador laughed sharply. "That's a risk we must take. We must have water."

The end of that night's journey brought them to the base of the mountains. There they stopped to fill their canteens at an all-night service station. The attendant paid no heed to them; he was occupied with a *gringo* car that drove in at the same moment. Its radiator was boiling over, and clouds of steam rose from under the hood.

Salvador found a gully off the road for them to sleep in, and the next evening they began their climb up the winding mountain road. Finally, at daybreak, they came into flat country.

This time they rested in a tiny box canyon to the right of the highway. Too weary to eat, Lupita fell asleep at

110

once. At nightfall, Salvador had to shake her awake. She found it hard to keep her eyes open while she ate. The climb up the mountains had been terrible. Sometimes she had felt like putting her hands under her knees to lift them up for the next step. How her legs and feet ached now, but she must walk much farther to reach Indio!

That night the two of them drifted like smoke through the twin towns of Beaumont and Banning, and the rising of the sun found them in the Mojave Desert. As the sun came up through a milky, fiery mist, a blue pickup truck came roaring down the highway behind them. It was the only car on the road.

The Torres children stopped for an instant to look around. "It is a truck," Salvador said. "*La migra* drives sedans. Keep on walking, Lupita."

As they began to move on, the pickup slowed its speed to stay behind them. The driver, a young *gringo*, started to yell, and so did his passenger, another youth. Suddenly the truck jumped off the road onto the shoulder where Lupita and Salvador were walking. The horn blared, and the two young men shouted again.

Robbers? More robbers! thought Lupita in panic.

"Run!" Salvador shouted, as he leaped onto the pebble-strewn sand below the road. Lupita fled after him, running through cresote bushes and burroweed to a side road leading into the desert.

To her horror, the pickup came in pursuit, jolting down the unpaved road behind them. The youths shouted and laughed. "Wetbacks. Hey, wetbacks! Run, run."

The driver didn't catch up to them or pass them. He and his companion stayed a distance behind and continued yelling. In spite of her terror, Lupita realized that the young men were playing with them. They meant to herd them like cattle. What would they do when they tired of their game?

All at once the desert road went over a sand dune. Below the dune a giant boulder blocked the roadway.

"*Lupita*," cried Salvador, as he fled behind the boulder.

An instant later Lupita crouched there too, wondering what the two *gringos* would do. She looked over her shoulder and saw miles of soft, gray-white sand. If they tried to drive the pickup behind the rock, it would get mired in the sand. But even without their car, the young men were dangerous. What terrible thing would happen now?

Lupita and Salvador didn't have long to wait. *Ping.* A bullet struck the top of the boulder and ricocheted off. For several minutes the two *gringos* shot at the boulder, guffawing in the distance.

Weeping, Lupita flattened herself against the rock. Salvador cursed continuously in Spanish. While he cursed, she prayed that the men would not come after them. What was to stop them? Who was to stop them?

But after a while she heard the pickup's motor start. It turned around and began to bump back along the road going toward the highway.

"Salvador, Salvador," Lupita wept, clinging to her brother.

"The devils have gone!" After a moment he added through clenched teeth, "We won't go back to the highway. They could be waiting there for us. Let's go down the road and find a place to rest."

"*Sí*, Salvador, *sí*. Don't go back to the highway yet."

The place they found some distance down the road was an abandoned prospector's cabin. It was an ugly little building without a front door, set in a landscape of distant, gray-brown mountains and flat, white-gray basins. The only color was some dark, spindly bushes and spiney cacti. The shack seemed haunted.

"I do not like it here," Lupita said, as they ate and drank.

Salvador shook his head. "*La migra* will not find us here, and the *gringos* cannot come because the sand is so soft. Go to sleep, Lupita."

But Lupita lay awake on the floor for a long time, listening to the daytime noises of the desert. She heard frightening bird shrieks and the dry sounds of something moving under the floorboards. Were animals living under there? When she put an eye to a knothole in the floor, she discovered two thick-bodied rattlesnakes, taking refuge from the fierce sun. Lupita shuddered, rolled over to Salvador's back, and held tightly to him. He did not awaken. She would warn him before they started out again in the evening, for the snakes would come out then too.

The next night she and Salvador walked through the luxurious desert resort city of Palm Springs. Once more they filled their canteens at a service station on the eastern edge of the town. The attendant was a middle-aged *pocho*. He asked them in Spanish, "What do you kids want?"

"Some water, *por favor*," answered Salvador.

"Help yourselves, *muchachos*. Where are you going? You can tell me. I won't call *la migra*."

Lupita looked at him in fright.

"To Indio," replied Salvador, more trusting than she.

"How far is it from here, *señor*?" Lupita asked.

"Thirty miles."

Thirty miles! *Ay de mí*! After all their walking and

climbing and running, they were little more than halfway there.

"Where did you start from?" the man asked.

"Colton, *señor.*"

The *pocho* shook his head. "That's a long way. You kids be careful. From here to Indio *la migra* watches the road for wetbacks like you."

Lupita understood the word *wetback*. Concha had explained that it came from the wet backs of Mexicans who stealthily crossed the Rio Grande. But she and Salvador had come from Tijuana. Yet they were wetbacks to the *pochos* and *gringos*!

"*Gracias*, we will be careful," Salvador said.

The man stared past Salvador at Lupita. Did he guess they had money? Did he plan to rob them? She saw that Salvador, though polite, was eager to leave.

But the man made no move toward them. He leaned on a gas pump and watched as they continued eastward.

Lupita and Salvador found another side road, and they slid down into a desert gully to sleep. As they slept, the *santana* wind came up, and they awoke to dust and stinging sand strangling them.

They walked, coughing, until just before dawn, when they spotted a road sign with *Indio* and the number *15* beside it. Lupita pointed it out to Salvador, who grunted. "*Sí*, fifteen miles. If we walk hard, we can be in Indio tomorrow morning."

"*Mañana*," echoed Lupita, leaning tiredly against the sign. What a long time away that was. She brightened a moment later, though. *La migra* had not caught them yet, and there was only one more night to travel.

They didn't find another gully, but Salvador did see an

114

old, abandoned car off the road. He slept in the front of it on the white-with-dust upholstery, and Lupita on the back seat. She knew he had taken the front so he could pretend the car belonged to him. Ah, Salvador! He liked all machines.

The next night was a cruel one. There were more automobiles on the road now, and any one of them could be *la migra*. When cars seemed to slow down, Lupita quickly followed Salvador off the shoulder into the desert. Five times they fled in this way and came out only when the car was out of sight.

Stumbling along behind Salvador, Lupita told herself that she must keep putting one foot in front of the other. All she could see were her own feet, plodding along as she counted *"Uno, dos, uno, dos."*

Life came down to one thing only now—keeping her feet moving on the road that led to Indio.

9

Two hours after the sun had risen, they reached Indio. They approached the western edge of the desert city and stood for a moment at a highway marker that read *Indio*. Salvador smiled at Lupita, who wearily grinned back at him. "Now we will find Aunt Consuelo's house," he said.

"How will we do that?"

"We will ask a *pocho*."

The city was just beginning to awaken. There were a few cars on the streets, but almost no people, and those they saw were pale-eyed *gringos*.

As they came to the center of town, Salvador said crossly, "Walk beside me on the sidewalk. Act like a *pocho* with nothing to fear."

They passed no one who appeared to be a Mexican-American until they had left the business district of still-closed offices, stores, and cafés. Finally they saw a pretty, dark-haired girl coming toward them. Brown-skinned, she wore white shoes, white trousers, and a white tunic.

"I think she is a *pocha*," Lupita whispered.

As the girl came abreast of them, Salvador took off his hat and said in Spanish, *"Linda mujer*, pretty lady, *por favor*, can you tell me where to find the house of Señora Consuelo García de Ruiz?"* In an aside, he asked Lupita, "What is her address?"

"Route *número uno*, box *número cuatro*."

The brunette stopped, looked at them, and said, "*Sí*, I know where route *número uno* is. I once lived there. Take that street." She pointed to the east, smiling at Lupita. "*Muchacho*, the word *route* means only the road a postman travels. Do you know what the word *box* means?"

"No, *señorita*."

"It is a *buzón* made out of metal and placed on a piece of wood beside the road."

"*Sí*, I have seen them."

"*Bueno*, look for the number four on the box, and that will be the house you want."

"*Gracias, gracias, señorita*." Lupita smiled. How kind this *pocha* was. She must know they were Mexicans, but she had said nothing. Looking at the white uniform, Lupita asked, "Are you a maid in a hotel here?"

"No, I am a nurse. *Adiós*, I must go to work now."

A nurse! What important work *pochas* did! How clever this young woman must be to have such a good job!

An hour later they had reached the end of the street the *pocha* had pointed out, and they turned onto a dirt road. There had been no mail boxes earlier, but now they could see a long line of black and silver ones set atop poles on each side.

The houses were small and drab, constructed of gray concrete blocks. There were no lawns, only brown dirt pockmarked with weeds. Could this be where Aunt

Consuelo lived with her rich husband? Lupita asked herself in wonderment. These little houses did not appear to be places where rich people lived. Could the lady have given them wrong directions?

Worried, Lupita read the number and names on each mailbox. At last she found a black box on the right side of the street that bore the name Hermilio Ruiz in white lettering. That was Aunt Consuelo's husband's name, Hermilio.

They had found her!

Lupita and Salvador stared at the house that stood behind the mailbox, then wordlessly looked at one another. This gray concrete house was a duplicate of the others they had seen on the dirt road. There were no flowers in front, nothing but a big, brown tumbleweed, which had been blown to one side of the front door.

"Come, Lupita," Salvador said sharply, and he went to the door and rapped.

A small girl dessed in a man's white undershirt opened the door and stared at them in puzzlement. "Mamá," she wailed, and went back inside the house, shutting the door behind her.

Moments later a heavy, barefoot, gray-haired woman opened the door again. She stood, filling the doorway, and looked at Salvador and Lupita, who had taken off the baseball cap to let her braids show.

"Aunt Consuelo?" Salvador asked tentatively.

All at once her eyes widened, and she drew in her breath.

"I am Salvador Torres," Salvador went on. "This is my sister, Lupita. We are the children of Señora Carmela García de Torres. We have come to you from Ensenada."

118

"Holy Mother." The woman breathed heavily. "I didn't think you would make it. *Sí*, I am Consuelo García de Ruiz."

"Aunt Consuelo," Lupita said, "we have walked through the mountains and the desert from Colton. We are very weary now. I wrote the letter from Mexico, for Mamá, your sister."

Consuelo sighed again, still not moving from the door. "My son Elvio wrote at once to your mother. I am sorry that you did not receive his letter in time. He said that it would be better if you did not come here."

"*Not come here?*" Lupita repeated, sensing Salvador stiffening next to her.

"*Sí*." Aunt Consuelo shook her head. "We are crowded in this house. I am not rich. We have been lying to your mother for a long time. My husband wanted my family in Mexico to believe we were rich. *Ay de mí*! Hermilio!" The woman pointed to her gray head. "Every gray hair here has its story." She finally backed away from the doorway. "Come in. After all, you are my sister's kids."

What a welcome this was, thought Lupita, feeling awkward and embarrassed. There were no embraces, no joy at all. They had walked many miles for very little.

The house smelled strongly of gas from a small stove that stood in one corner of the main room. Lupita saw at a glance that the furnishings were poor: a sagging sofa with a red-and-green blanket thrown over it, a closed, unpainted cupboard, a kitchen sink, four wooden chairs and a table, and against the far wall a single bed occupied by small children covered with a blanket. Through open doors Lupita spied two other bedrooms with people in the beds. Was Uncle Hermilio still in bed then?

"Sit down, sit down," ordered Consuelo. After they had seated themselves, she asked, seemingly without embarrassment, "Do you have a dollar? It is the end of the month, and I have no money left. If you have a dollar, I will send Catarina to the store to buy milk for breakfast."

After a surprised glance at Lupita, Salvador fished a dollar bill out of his pocket and handed it to Consuelo. She took it and called, "Get up, Catarina, I need you!"

A thin, fully dressed girl came out of the bedroom on the left. She rubbed her eyes, stared at Lupita and Salvador in astonishment, and asked, "Who are these people, Mamá?"

"They are your cousins from Ensenada."

"Where is Papá?" asked the girl, still staring at Lupita and Salvador.

"Not here. He went out again last night. Here is a dollar. Run to the all-night market, and buy us some milk before you go to school." After another curious, unsmiling glance at Salvador and Lupita, Catarina ran out the open front door.

Lupita, who sagged with fatigue in her chair, watched her aunt lumber over to the bed in the corner and grab the two small children in it. "Get up. Get to the bathroom," she ordered. Then she went into the other rooms and awoke the children there.

Lupita shivered. This was not a loving house. She and Salvador were not welcome. Her aunt had not wanted them to come to Indio at all. What were they doing in this cold place?

She shivered and saw that she was surrounded by children, staring wide-eyed at her and Salvador as they dressed themselves on the living-room floor. Their mother pointed to the littlest of them and said, "Esmeralda, the youngest. This is Irela, Pascual, and Juan. Elvio is your age, Lupita. Catarina is eleven."

Not one of the Ruiz cousins said a word. They stood silently near their mother. Suddenly Esmeralda called out happily as Catarina burst through the doorway with a big carton of milk.

"The milk is a gift from my sister and me," Salvador said to the group. No one responded.

The children ate their flour tortillas and milk standing up, but Lupita and Salvador sat at the table. When they were finished, the Ruiz children silently left the house except for the oldest, Elvio. He went into one of the bedrooms with his mother, where they spoke in low tones. Then he came out, and with another glance at his cousins he stalked outside, shutting the door behind him.

Aunt Consuelo sat down and poured herself some coffee from a pot she must have brewed the night before. "My kids go out now to wait for the buses that take them to their schools." She sipped the black brew. "Are you tired? Are you sleepy?"

"Sí, Aunt Consuelo. We are very tired," Salvador answered. His voice sounded far away to Lupita. Her eyes kept closing in spite of her efforts to keep them open. As if from a distance, she heard her aunt say, "I can see that you are. Go to bed then. I'll wake you when Hermilio comes home."

"Does Uncle Hermilio work nights?" Salvador asked politely.

"Holy Mother, no!" Aunt Consuelo answered in a scornful tone. Startled, Lupita opened her eyes and saw her aunt pressing her hand to her chest. "Because you did not get Elvio's letter in time, my heart is heavy. Why didn't you stay in Colton?"

"*La migra* came where we worked," replied Salvador, and he told her about their experiences at the café.

Aunt Consuelo nodded. "*Sí, la migra.* I know of *la migra*, but it cannot touch me because I am married to an American. What concerns me is *la ayuda.* These days it is *la ayuda* that puts food into our mouths and pays our rent."

"What is *la ayuda?*" Salvador asked, as Lupita's eyes closed once more.

"The welfare. Without *la ayuda* we could not live. I cannot earn enough to feed all of us."

"Is Uncle Hermilio out so early looking for work?"

"No. Last evening he went to drink beer with his friends in the *cantina.*" Consuelo answered grimly. "I know his ways by now. From the *cantina* he went to the house of a friend to play cards. Hermilio is nothing now. He has trouble with his back and his lungs. All he can do is go to the *cantina*, play cards, and cough." Consuelo pulled herself up. "Now you two go to bed and get some sleep. But, *por favor*, give me another dollar to buy some rice for tonight. I want my sister's children to stay and have supper with us."

Lupita looked at Salvador and saw him reach slowly into his pocket and give Consuelo another dollar. She stuffed the bill into the side pocket of her long pink gown. Lupita felt her aunt's hand on her shoulder. "Ah, go to bed, you kids. I don't have to work today. I'll lie down for a while myself before I buy the rice. Take any bed you want."

Lupita got up, her head reeling, and headed for the

room on the right. Before she went inside, Salvador caught her and whispered, "Don't tell anyone here how much money we have with us, Lupita."

With her eyes on Consuelo, Lupita asked, "Do you think our aunt's family would rob us?"

"No, but they can go on asking us for money."

"What will we do, Salvador?" Lupita's eyes searched his face, haggard with fatigue.

"Sleep while we can. When we get up, I'll make up my mind what to do."

Lupita had no idea how long she slept. She awoke to the sound of her name. "Lupita, Lupita." It was still daylight. She lifted her head, and the little bedroom spun around her. For a moment she sat on the side of the bed, and then she got up and went out into the living room.

Aunt Consuelo sat at the table with a small man in a blue-cotton shirt and trousers. He had a thick body, heavy shoulders, a long, bony face, and thinning hair. As he looked at Lupita, he coughed. Uncle Hermilio! Under heavy lids, his eyes were red and bloodshot.

He examined Lupita closely, scanning her carefully from head to toe. Suddenly he said in a deep voice, "Another kid? When we have six of our own, your sister sends us more. Where is the boy? Why doesn't he come out?"

"He'll come out soon. You know that boys sleep harder than girls. Lupita, go sit on the sofa." Aunt Consuelo looked toward the bedroom and gestured to Salvador, who stood in the doorway. "Come and sit by your sister." She turned to Hermilio. "I have already told you that this boy worked in Colton as a dishwasher and Lupita as a maid in a motel. If they found jobs in Colton, they can find work here."

Hermilio Ruiz looked at Salvador and Lupita. "Have you still got the forged social-security cards you bought in Colton?"

"Sí, we have them with us," Salvador answered. Lupita raised her eyebrows at her brother's insolent tone.

"Then you can work and find yourselves some place to live," Hermilio grumbled and turned away.

They would be leaving here then. Lupita was not surprised, but Hermilio's ugly manner stung her. "We have already sent money to Mamá," she volunteered. "Salvador and I expect to work wherever we can. We want to help Mamá and our brothers and sisters."

"*Silencio!*" Salvador hissed. He didn't care for this man's good opinion, and he resented her attempt to impress him.

Suddenly Aunt Consuelo hit the table with the palm of her hand. "Hermilio, I have just had an idea. These kids are not going away to pay rent somewhere else! They are going to stay here with us! We'll *make* room for them. They can live and work here and pay us for their food and beds. The little ones can sleep on the floor in the living room. We do not need to tell welfare that they are living with us and paying rent. Salvador and Lupita will cost *la ayuda* nothing."

"They are wetbacks, Consuelo," Hermilio mumbled. "I don't want *la migra* making trouble for me."

"Hermilio, *la migra* has no reason to come here. Have there ever been any wetbacks in this house before? No."

Hermilio coughed and once more turned his gaze on Lupita and Salvador. After a moment he nodded. "Okay.

124

But *la migra* does raid where people work. It raided a *cantina* on the other side of town night before last."

Lupita tensed herself, but Uncle Hermilio went on. "I think these two had better start work in the fields. There are fewer questions asked there. Tell anybody who asks that they are my niece and nephew from Texas and they forgot their social-security cards." Suddenly Hermilio chuckled and pointed to his wife. "This old woman of mine, she will look after you. Have you two ever worked in the fields before?"

"No," Salvador said.

"I promise you fisherman's kids that once you do you won't forget what it's like. I never will. . . ." His voice trailed off into a coughing fit.

"Lupita and I can work," Salvador assured him.

"*Sí*, we can work hard," Lupita added. She knew that she should say *gracias*, but the word stuck in her throat like a fishbone.

"How much rent did you pay in Colton?" Aunt Consuelo asked.

"One hundred forty dollars a month for the two of us."

"That will be all right here too." Aunt Consuelo smiled at her husband, who nodded at her, then looked away out the window.

10

The beans and rice Aunt Consuelo cooked that evening were tasty, but eating was no pleasure for Lupita. No one at the table spoke, and Uncle Hermilio paid attention only to a little radio he had brought with him. He kept it tuned to an English-speaking station.

Elvio explained over the noise of the radio, "Papá listens to all of the *gringo* sports. When he went to school, he played on the baseball team." Suddenly Elvio asked Salvador. "Are you going to the fields tomorrow with Mamá?"

"Sí," Salvador said glumly.

Catarina spoke up. "Sometimes on Saturdays Elvio goes along. How long did you go to school in Mexico? We go for twelve years." She made a sour face.

Twelve years! Lupita stared at her yellow plastic plate. Her cousins were lucky to be able to get so much education. *Ay de mi!* Even if Papá had lived, no one in her family would have enjoyed so much school.

"Don't you know any English at all?" Catarina inquired.

"No," Salvador said.

"The other maid where I worked said she would teach me what she knew," Lupita added, "but she never found the time."

"Oh" was all Catarina said.

Suddenly Salvador asked, "Aunt Consuelo, when do we go to the fields?"

"Before the sun comes up. Fidencio comes to get me in his truck at five o'clock in the morning."

"Who is Fidencio?"

Aunt Consuelo jerked her thumb at her husband, who was hunched over the radio. "Hermilio's brother. He is a good worker, that old Fidencio. He has a telephone in his house, so the *gringos* who own the fields call him when they need people. Fidencio came to tell me last night that there is squash in the valley this week." She ticked off on her fingers. "After that comes asparagus and cabbage and broccoli, and then the lemons and onions and radishes. Then, the grapefruit and the oranges, sweet corn, and grapes. Fidencio knows all the growers. He keeps me working almost all year long."

"Will this Señor Fidencio want us to pay him to find us work? We had to pay a man in Colton." Salvador's tone was sharp.

"Not Fidencio," Aunt Consuelo answered.

Salvador's expression became less sour. "What are workers paid in the fields?"

"Two dollars an hour for you kids."

Lupita sucked in her breath in dismay. She had made more as a chambermaid.

Salvador glowered. "That is less than Lupita and I were paid in Colton."

Aunt Consuelo shrugged. "That is what the growers pay the young ones who harvest for them."

"Sí," Elvio agreed. "That is what I am paid on Saturdays."

When Salvador lapsed into a glum silence, Lupita asked, "Aunt Consuelo, could you teach me some English words as we work in the fields?"

Aunt Consuelo, Elvio, and Catarina began to laugh. Uncle Hermilio switched off his radio and asked Elvio something in English. Then he laughed too.

Finally Elvio explained, "Mamá knows almost no English. We always have to speak Spanish to her."

"How can that be?" Lupita asked in wonder. "Our mother told us Aunt Consuelo came here twenty years ago."

"Sí, I came over and got a job as a maid. All I ever learned from the *gringa* I worked for were words like *vacuum cleaner, broom* and *mop, washing machine* and *clothesline,* things like that. She warned me not to go to night school because she was afraid *la migra* would catch me there. I worked for her for six years. Then I met Hermilio at a dance, and we got married. We always spoke Spanish to one another, and I did not go to work again. A few years ago I began to work in the fields where no one speaks anything but Spanish. I have no need of English. Neither will either one of you."

Lupita glanced at Salvador, wondering what he thought of Aunt Consuelo's story, but he was looking out the window at the darkening sky.

"Don't you go to the market?"

"Sí, Lupita, but one of the children goes with me." Consuelo laughed. "Even if I do go alone, there is always someone there who speaks Spanish. It is not hard to live here without knowing English. Our doctor is a *pocho*. The people of *la ayuda* speak Spanish too."

Suddenly Salvador turned his head. "Once Lupita wanted to become a *profesora*. That is why she talks of learning English when she has no need of it. Lupita likes to study. She likes books."

While Elvio and Catarina and Aunt Consuelo chuckled, Lupita gave her brother an angry look. He didn't need to make fun of her, even if he was unhappy.

All at once Lupita became aware of Irela Ruiz, the second oldest girl. She stood at Lupita's elbow and plucked at her sleeve. Softly, so no one else could hear, Irela said, "I like my *profesora*."

Lupita stared at the unsmiling girl, who looked about eight years old. Her large, dark eyes gave Lupita no hint of friendliness. Suddenly she spun around and darted out through the open door into the twilight to join her younger brothers and sisters.

That night Lupita slept with Catarina, and Salvador shared the bed in the living room with small Juan.

When it was still dark, Lupita was awakened by a bright light. Aunt Consuelo, holding a flashlight, whispered, "Come on. Your brother is up. Do not step on Esmeralda and Pascual when we come into the living room. We will eat when we get to the fields."

On Aunt Consuelo's orders Lupita had slept fully dressed. Now she put on her shoes and stumbled through the house into the darkness outside. Salvador waited there. Following the beam of Consuelo's flashlight, they walked to the roadside to wait beside the Ruiz mailbox.

Lupita shivered and pulled the collar of Salvador's jacket around her ears. After a while she heard the sound of an automobile in the distance and soon she could see one headlight. Her aunt, who wore a man's straw hat, shone the flashlight on the road, and an old, battered brown truck drew up to the mailbox and stopped.

A deep voice called from the driver's seat, "*Hola*, Consuelo, what have you got there with you?"

"Two of my sister's kids from Mexico, or maybe they are Hermilio's relations from Texas."

The man laughed. "Okay. Tell them to get in the back of the truck with the others."

Aunt Consuelo held the flashlight so they could see to crawl into the rear of the truck.

Five people sat there, all shabbily dressed and wearing straw hats—two middle-aged men and three middle-aged women. They looked at Salvador and Lupita curiously, but no one said anything.

Chilled by the early-morning air and afraid of the day ahead, Lupita started to touch the cross at her throat. She had forgotten it was gone. As soon as she got more money, she would have to buy another. A new cross would never be as precious as Papá's, but it would be better than none at all.

Before long the truck left the highway, turned onto a dirt road, and then onto another before it bounced to a stop beside a wooden building set in the middle of flat fields. While there still was not enough light to see the crops, Lupita could make out the silhouettes of other trucks and people standing about.

Aunt Consuelo got out, banged the truck door shut, and cried, "Lupita, Salvador, come with me. I'll take you to the boss."

The boss was a big, redheaded *gringo*, who sat at a table inside the shack. The overhead lights were so bright they made Lupita's eyes ache. The *gringo* gestured toward the Torres children and asked in harsh, queer-sounding Spanish, "What have you got here, Consuelo?"

"My husband's niece and nephew from Texas," she told him. "They have cards, but they forgot to bring them along. You know how kids are!"

While Lupita froze to her spot on the floor, the *gringo* looked her and Salvador up and down. He grunted. "They forgot, huh? I've heard that before. But I suppose they can harvest squash. What is your name?" he asked Salvador, reaching for a piece of paper.

"Joe Ruiz," replied Aunt Consuelo quickly. "This is his sister María."

"Ruiz and Ruiz, eh?" The *gringo* wrote down the names and said, "All right, that's all for now."

"*Sí*, Boss, *gracias*. They'll be very good workers. You'll see."

Aunt Consuelo herded Lupita and Salvador outside to where another man was handing out cardboard boxes. "There is food inside the boxes, food for now and later too," she said.

"How long do we work here?" Salvador asked.

"Until the boss tells us to stop. One or two o'clock."

"What are we to do?"

"Go find Fidencio. He will show you. He's brought many workers here and knows what the *gringos* want."

"What does Señor Fidencio look like?" Lupita asked. "We have not seen his face."

"He has hair the color of milk." Consuelo waved her hand and walked over to talk to some women standing in line for food.

By now there was light enough to see the faces of the men who had gathered together beside the shack. The white-haired man must be Señor Fidencio. He was long-faced like his brother, Hermilio, but there the resemblance ended. Fidencio was laughing with one of the other men and playfully pretending to jab at him with his fists.

Trailed by Lupita, Salvador went up to the group and waited to be noticed.

After a minute Fidencio Ruiz looked over. "Ah, you're the kids Consuelo brought. Did you ever box down in Mexico, kid?" he asked Salvador.

"No, Señor Fidencio."

"That's too bad. Boxing, that's one good way for a kid to get ahead. Joining the United States Army or Navy is another."

"Not for a wetback like me, *señor*," Salvador said.

"No." Señor Fidencio's face changed, growing thoughtful. Then he smiled again. "Long ago I used to be a boxer in the Army."

Salvador nodded. "Aunt Consuelo said you would show us what we are to do. We have never worked in the fields before. Our father was a fisherman."

Fidencio led them away from the other men. "I see you have your boxes. *Bueno*. After we eat, follow me into the field."

Lupita opened the box of food the *gringo* had given her. Inside were canned orange juice and some hard, brown doughnuts. They were dry and tasteless. The sandwiches in their waxed-paper packets were for mid-morning.

When she and Salvador had finished eating, Fidencio came back from where he had been sitting among the men. "Come with me."

132

Lupita watched him pick up a wooden box set along the edge of the field. Salvador grabbed a box too, and so did she. The box was light.

The crop to be harvested was summer squash—a small, scallop-edged, pale-green vegetable that grew close to the ground.

Fidencio bent over, took hold of a squash, and broke it away from its stem. Then he put it into the box and, lifting the green leaves, began to hunt for squash nearby. When he had filled his box, he carried it to the end of the row and set it down next to a stack of empty boxes. Lupita watched him take the wire handle off the full box and fasten it to one of the empty ones. Carrying it, he returned to the row in which he had been picking.

Before he bent over again, he grinned at her. "Do what I just did. Be sure to pick all of the squash in each row you work. After a while the boss will bring a truck to pick up the full boxes and take them to the market."

"*Sí, señor.*" Carrying her box, Lupita walked to the end of the sixty-foot row Fidencio had pointed out. It was six rows ahead of him.

At first, she found hunting among the leaves and along the ground for the small, green squash not difficult, but at the end of the second hour she began to understand why Uncle Hermilio had said they wouldn't forget the fields.

Each time she straightened up to carry a full box to the end of the row, her back felt as if someone had hit her with a stick. Kneading it did not ease the pain. Her neck and shoulders ached too, but *ay de mí* her hands! Twisting hundreds of squash from their stems was making cramped claws of them, and her fingers were raw with broken blisters.

As the bright October sun rose in the sky, the heat became unbearable for Lupita. She perspired more and more heavily. First, she took off Salvador's jacket and tied it around her hips; then she fished out the baseball cap she had left in the pocket.

Lupita quickly realized why the pickers all wore straw hats, because her wool baseball cap was unbearably hot. She felt as though someone had poured scalding water on her head. Sweat ran into her eyes, blinding her. When she wiped it off with her hand, her face became streaked with yellow-brown dirt. Salvador's old shirt clung to her, and as she twisted the vegetables from their stems, she felt her back begin to itch. She didn't know if it itched from the rivulets of sweat or from the ants and other insects she spied among the squash.

Holy Mother! And she had thought lifting the mattresses in Señor Elfren's motel was hard work.

Lupita glanced behind her and saw her aunt harvesting, never straightening up. Several rows away old Fidencio was doing the same. How fast those two picked! She stood up and focused with difficulty on Salvador. He was standing too at that moment, holding his hand to the small of his back. He looked around and saw her. Even at that distance, Lupita could see his black scowl. He shook his head and bent again to his work.

Lupita passed the remainder of the morning in a stupor of weariness. When the boss blew a whistle at ten, she collapsed beside her half-filled box and numbly ate her sandwiches. She could hardly taste the cheese and the bread. All she wanted was more cool water from the water cart. She had taken a drink every time it came around, and now she drank deeply again.

At one o'clock Lupita felt scarcely able to make her way out of her row. Somehow she got her envelope of cash and stumbled over to Señor Fidencio's truck.

She noted how angry Salvador looked as he got into the truck a minute later, but she was too tired to talk. Sitting down next to her, he hissed, "My back hurts! I hate this work! I liked the dishwasher better."

Lupita forced herself to speak. "Salvador, I do not like this work either, but *la migra* did not come here today."

"That does not mean that *la migra* will never come here," he grumbled. "*Dios*, I hate this kind of work!"

Lupita touched his arm with her raw fingers. "Perhaps it will be easier harvesting the other things that grow here. Perhaps picking fruit from trees will be more pleasant."

"*Mañana*? Always Lupita *Mañana*," he muttered. Then he added, "We must use ladders for trees. We can fall off." He shook off her hand.

All at once one of the women, who had been watching them, asked, "Do you and your sister go to church here in Indio?"

"We came here only yesterday," Salvador answered sullenly.

"You should go, *muchacho*. Señor Fidencio has a club for young men there. They have *fiestas*, good times."

Lupita snatched at the idea. "Salvador, you should go to Mass!"

"What about you?" he asked, still sullen.

"I cannot yet. Remember, I left my dress behind in Colton."

He sighed. "I suppose I can go to church."

"*Sí*, and I will get another dress. But first we will send more money to Mamá." Lupita hesitated. "I won't write of *la migra* driving us away. I will say that we are happy in Indio and that we have work."

Salvador gave her a tight smile. "So, more lies will come out of the Ruiz house."

"Salvador, why should we make Mamá more unhappy than she already is?"

"You are right, Lupita. You take care of it. We will send her as much as we can." He spoke with his eyes closed, leaning back against the side of the truck. As Fidencio went onto another road, Salvador wincing, bounced against the hard metal and cursed under his breath.

"Will you write Mamá what very fine work Uncle Hermilio and Aunt Consuelo found for us?" he muttered through clenched teeth.

"No, you know I will not." Lupita averted her eyes from his angry face. She was too exhausted to say any more.

11

The next morning, Saturday, Señor Fidencio came once more. Aunt Consuelo climbed into the truck's cab, and aching Lupita got into the rear with Salvador and Elvio. The same five harvesters were there, and Elvio talked and joked with them all, sometimes in English but mostly in Spanish.

When there was a pause in the conversation, Lupita ventured to speak to the woman across from her. "Señora, remember what you said yesterday? I would like to go to Mass tomorrow, but I do not have a dress."

The woman's voice came out of the darkness. "Your aunt has daughters. Wear one of their dresses."

Elvio chuckled. "Skinny as she is, Lupita is too big for their dresses." Then he added, "I suppose she could wear one of Mamá's, but no one would be able to find her in it." Elvio fell on his side, laughing. "Salvador, is your mother fat too?"

While Lupita's face burned in embarrassment, Salvador said curtly, "No." Then he asked, "How do we get to church?"

"Uncle Fidencio takes us there in his truck," Elvio replied, still giggling. "We'll go out in it tonight, too."

"Tonight?"

"Sí. After supper he's taking Catarina and me to the movie in town."

"Elvio, you should take your cousins from Mexico with you," the woman on the other side said.

"But we will not understand anything," Lupita protested.

Elvio chuckled. "Don't worry, Lupita, you will understand what the actors say. The theater we are going to has films in Spanish. I will ask Uncle Fidencio if you can come."

Lupita felt her brother's hand and squeezed his fingers. He returned the pressure. They were going to the movies!

In spite of her stiffness and sore hands, Lupita's spirits lifted as the dawn approached. Sí, she would buy another dress and shoes to wear to church as soon as she could. The dawn sky was a pale rosy pink. As the truck jolted along, Lupita dreamed of a rose-pink dress. She would buy pink ribbons for the ends of her braids, too.

Harvesting the remainder of the summer squash crop was no less tiring than it had been the day before. Her shoulders, back, and hands ached when she stopped for lunch, and they hurt even more by the end of the working day. Traveling from Tijuana had made her dislike Brussels sprouts; now she hated summer squash as well! As they rode home, she vowed that she would never eat this queer green vegetable either.

Catarina had supper almost ready when they returned. Consuelo smiled and asked, "Are you helping tonight so I will give you money to go to the cinema?"

"Of course, Mamá," Catarina replied impishly.

"Where is your father?"

"I don't know. He went out again this morning with the man who lives next door."

Aunt Consuelo nodded. "Then we won't see him until tomorrow, I suppose. *Bueno*, I'll rest on the sofa tonight and listen to the music on the radio." Suddenly she touched the shoulder of the child nearest her. "How does that suit you, Irela, to listen to the radio?"

Irela said nothing, but looked mournfully at her mother. Lupita understood. Irela wanted to go to the cinema too, but was afraid to ask.

"Salvador and Lupita are going to the movies with us. They said that they would pay their own way," Elvio reported.

"What did Fidencio say? He did not mention it to me."

"He said okay."

"*Okay*." Lupita echoed the English word in her mind.

"It only means *sí*," Catarina told her, reading the question on her face.

Lupita hesitated a moment. Then, looking at her brother, she asked, "Will it be dangerous for Salvador and me to go to the cinema?"

"Don't worry. Go. If *la migra* comes, say that you are Joe and María Ruiz from Texas. Go to church as Joe and María too," Consuelo advised.

Lupita pointed to the shirt and trousers she wore. "Will they let me inside in these?"

Everyone but Salvador and the youngest Ruiz cousin laughed at her question. "Don't worry about the cinema and how you look," Elvio replied. "You should see how some of the rich *gringa* girls dress. They look worse than you do."

All at once Lupita became aware of Irela looking at her, serious as ever. On an impulse she said, "Aunt Consuelo, may I take Irela to the cinema with me? I will buy her a ticket."

Aunt Consuelo chuckled, reached out to Irela, and yanked at one side of her long hair. "Sí, Irela can go then. Would you like that, Irela?"

"Sí, Mamá." After a swift glance at Lupita, Irela buried her face in the folds of her mother's skirt.

Though Indio by night was brightly lit, Lupita found it little like Tijuana and much like Colton. Except for the sounds of traffic, there was not much noise. Señor Fidencio parked his truck behind the theater and led the way to the ticket booth. His white-haired wife accompanied him. He bought tickets for both of them, and then Elvio, holding Salvador's and Lupita's money, bought tickets for the rest.

They all sat together on the ground floor and watched a story Lupita already knew. It was the old Mexican fairy tale of the Queen of the Clouds and the witch. Lupita had told it many times to her little sisters and brothers, but watching it now made her forget her aches and pains. Irela sat between Señor Fidencio and his wife and did not take her eyes from the screen once.

The next morning Lupita sat down to write a letter to her mother. The house was empty and quiet; everyone had gone to church. Uncle Hermilio had not returned. Lupita wrote slowly and carefully with a pencil stub, trying to give the impression that they were welcome and had found good jobs. It was hard not knowing what Elvio had written earlier.

After Lupita signed the letter with words of love, she folded a ten- and a five-dollar bill inside the paper. Then she put the letter into the envelope, sealed it tightly, and addressed it to Ensenada. She placed four one-dollar bills on top, money for Uncle Hermilio to register it tomorrow.

When she was through, she went outside to sit on the front doorstep and enjoy the morning sunshine. Lupita looked at her black-rimmed, broken fingernails resting on her sweat-soaked trousers. How her appearance would shock Mamá, who worked in a crisp yellow jacket in Señor Aguilar's beautiful hotel.

When Salvador and the others came home from church, Señor Fidencio, his wife, and a liquid-eyed, black-haired boy a bit taller than Salvador came into the house with them. The young man was elegantly dressed in black trousers, black high-heeled boots, and a black-and-purple jacket with gold-colored satin sleeves. In one hand he carried a gleaming brown guitar with a long scarlet cord and tassels.

"That is Lucio," Salvador told Lupita quietly, once Señor Fidencio and his wife had sat down on the sofa. "Aunt Consuelo asked him to have coffee with us, and Señor Fidencio stopped and bought cakes for everyone."

"Who is Lucio?" Lupita whispered, staring at the finely dressed youth.

"Señor Fidencio's grandson. He studies in a school to be a mechanic and works at night as a dishwasher in a café." Salvador's eyes were fixed on Lucio. "He plays the guitar and sings. Today he played the guitar in church.

After they all had coffee and pink-frosted cupcakes, Aunt Consuelo requested that Lucio sing something. He picked up his guitar and began to play.

Lupita soon felt disappointed. Though he had a good tenor, he sang only *gringo* songs, and Lupita couldn't understand them. She looked around to see if Salvador felt the same way, but he was listening raptly.

After a while, Lucio asked what people would like to hear. When everyone had made a request, Lupita asked, "*Por favor*, play 'La Paloma.' It is my favorite."

"No, not that old one," Lucio said coldly. "I am tired of it."

Lupita shrank back. He had played "La Golondrina" for Aunt Consuelo, another old song. Now he started to strum another tune, which prompted Elvio and Catarina to get off the floor and start a queer sort of twisting, arm-waving dance.

When Señor Fidencio and his wife rose to leave, Lupita saw Lucio motion with his finger to Salvador to follow him outside.

When Salvador returned, he looked happy, happier than Lupita had seen him in a long time. "Lupita, I think Lucio Ruiz is going to turn out to be a friend to me." Salvador was grinning. "You should know, Lupita, that he doesn't like the name Lucio. He asked me to call him Lucky from now on."

"What does that word mean, Salvador?"

"I don't know. Elvio," Salvador called out, "what does *lucky* mean in English?"

"*Afortunado*, that's close enough."

"Do his mother and father live here in Indio also?" Lupita asked.

Salvador laughed. "They live here, but Lucky does not live with them."

"He lives with Señor Fidencio then?"

"Not him." Salvador smiled strangely. "Lucky lives with other *pochos* he knows, friends of his. One of them plays the trumpet and another the guitar. Lucky said that he only came to church today to please his grandfather. He would rather have stayed home and worked on his car. He's going to have to borrow his grandfather's truck to take his sweetheart to the *gringo* movie tonight." Salvador looked at Lupita intently. "No one goes with them to keep them company. The *gringo* way with sweethearts is to be alone."

"No one goes with them?" echoed Lupita, astonished.

Salvador shook his head in admiration. "Ah, these *pochos*! Lucky says he will come get me next Saturday night in his car. It will be fixed by then. I told him about Captain Ortega and Dorotea, and he said that kind of thing would never happen here in the United States. He said Dorotea is a prisoner and that should not be. He said if Dorotea had any courage and if she had truly loved me, she would have run away from her father and come with us. He says that it doesn't make any difference if the girl's family is rich and the boy's family is poor here. Love is all that counts."

Stunned, Lupita leaned against the wall. "Lucio certainly said very much to you, Salvador!"

"Sí, he talks fast. He made friends with me right away. He said he was glad to see somebody near his own age in the back of the truck. Lucky promises to try to help me. He told me that things would turn out okay for me if I listened to him."

"Okay?" Lupita repeated. She was tempted to call her brother's new friend Lucio Mañana, but that would only have made Salvador angry.

143

After a moment Lupita said, "But, Salvador, you do not have the fine clothing to go out with Lucio Ruiz!"

Salvador shrugged. "Lucky says a *pocho* who lived with him and his friends joined the Army last month. He left some of his clothes behind to be given away. Lucky said the *pocho* was my size, so he is going to gather up the clothes and give them to Señor Fidencio for me."

"Someone else's clothing?" Lupita recalled Salvador's reaction when she had begged in Tijuana. This was also taking charity, wasn't it?

Salvador pointed to Papá's black-and-white coat, which he had flung over the back of a chair. "That's someone else's too, Lupita!" he said sharply.

"But it was Papá's!" Lupita cried, shocked.

Rather than argue in front of the Ruizs, she turned and headed outside. At the door she looked back ruefully at her brother. He was not coming after her. He sat hunched over at the table, angrily drumming with his fingers.

All at once he said to the room at large, "Lucky told me that working in the fields is the worst kind of work he knows. When he was just a kid, he went there a time or two, but he didn't stay with it. His father got a good job as a janitor in a school, and afterward nobody in his house went to the fields again. He said that kind of work is for old men and women and kids."

"And wetbacks!" Elvio added.

How like Elvio to make that remark. Lupita went outside and shut the door behind her on the laughter of the Ruiz cousins and her brother's fury.

12

Monday came and once more Lupita, Salvador, and Aunt Consuelo went out in Fidencio's truck. This time he took them in a different direction, and they harvested zucchini squash. They didn't snap them off by hand, but used metal cutters. By quitting time Lupita's hands ached as much as before, and her fingers were blistered in new places, a cruel gift of the cutters.

She felt better, however, when she got home and caught sight of the little white paper on the table that proved Hermilio had sent the letter as he had promised. He had also kept the change from Lupita's four dollars, but she had expected he might.

The next day, Tuesday, was extremely hot, one of those freakish humid days that sometimes strike Indio late in October. No morning breezes cooled Lupita as she labored in the same field as the day before. Perspiration poured off her body, streaming into her eyes, making her long for the water she carried with her in a plastic bottle.

Now and then she straightened up to ease her back,

wipe the sweat from her eyes with her shirt sleeve, and take a long drink from the bottle. To refocus her eyes, she looked out over the field before she bent once more to cut the deep-green vegetables from their vines.

Near noon, the sun blazing directly overhead, Lupita rose for yet another drink. This time the warm water made her feel sick to her stomach. She gazed out over the field, which shimmered in a haze of smog and heat. Fighting nausea, she looked ahead for Salvador, Aunt Consuelo, and Señor Fidencio. They were stooped over, harvesting. Between her and them were the other pickers from Señor Fidencio's truck.

Suddenly Lupita's eyes riveted on the woman nearest her, some three rows ahead. The middle-aged *pocha* was also standing up, her body swaying. As Lupita watched, she put her hand to her chest and sank to her knees, crying out softly.

What should she do? Lupita asked herself in panic. Aunt Consuelo would know! Lupita put down her water bottle and began to run, leaping over the rows. As she passed the sick woman's row, Lupita glanced over and saw that she was bending forward and vomiting.

"Tia Consuelo! Tia Consuelo!" Lupita cried, running.

Consuelo heard and stood up, turning around to look about. Lupita ran up, panting, and pointed to where the other woman knelt in her row.

"Elena. It is Elena!" Consuelo cried, as she recognized who she was.

Lupita said swiftly, "I saw her go down. Shall I get the boss?"

"No!" Her aunt's voice was firm. "Stay away from him and his shed. Get Fidencio instead."

146

"Sí."

While her aunt started toward Elena, Lupita hurried through the rows to Señor Fidencio. He had just filled a box with zucchini and was carrying it to the edge of the field. When he saw Lupita coming, he stopped.

Her heart racing, Lupita gasped out, "Señor, it is the woman they call Elena. I saw her fall down. I went to Aunt Consuelo, and she said to come to you."

"Elena? Take my box to the end of this row, little one."

Lupita did as he ordered, then ran along the side of the field to Elena's row. Her aunt was sitting on the ground, and Elena was leaning against her shoulder. The front of Elena's cotton dress was dark with perspiration as she gasped to fill her lungs with air.

Señor Fidencio, kneeling beside the two women, touched Elena's forehead with his hand, then her heavy, bare arms. "Elena, your skin is very wet, but you have no fever. Are you dizzy?" he asked gently.

"Sí, very dizzy and sick to my stomach. I felt so weak I fell down. Then I threw up."

He nodded. "The sickness that comes with the heat. I have had it myself. It can be very dangerous. The boss will call for an ambulance to take you to the hospital."

"No, no, Fidencio!" Elena struggled away from Consuelo Ruiz's shoulder, stretching out her hand. She caught his wrist and pleaded, "Fidencio, *por favor*, help me to your truck. I can lie down in the back. I need to sleep for a time. I'll be all right. I've had this before too. Do not ask the boss for an ambulance. Tell him I have the flu. Give me some of my water and the salt shaker in my pocket. I think I didn't put in enough salt this morning. *Ay de mí!* Do not let the boss call for the ambulance! *La*

147

migra will find me, and I have been here so long now."
Exhausted, Elena fell back onto Consuelo's shoulder.

La migra? thought Lupita. This woman was a Mexican
like herself and as afraid of *la migra* as she was!

"Lupita, go back to your row," Fidencio ordered. "After
we take Señora Elena to the truck, I'll finish her row."

Obediently Lupita went back over the rows and picked
up her clippers. Before she began to snip off squash again,
she watched Señor Fidencio and Aunt Consuelo help the
staggering Elena to the old truck parked a distance away
under the lacy pepper trees. Looking away, Lupita sought
out her brother. There he was ahead of her, sitting down
and harvesting.

As she started to work, Lupita wondered how many
other harvesters in this field also were wetbacks. How
many others were as constantly afraid as she was? Now
she had a new fear for Salvador and herself. She was
afraid of an illness or an accident that could force them
into a hospital.

Elena was not in the back of the truck the next morning when Lupita and Salvador climbed in. One of the
other women told them in the darkness, "Señora Elena is
resting today. She will not go to the fields with us this
week, but she is feeling much better."

Before Lupita could say she was pleased, the woman
went on. "Salvador, do you see the big box here beside
me?"

"*Sí,* I see it."

"Fidencio says that it contains clothing for you. It is
from his grandson, Lucio."

Lupita tensed as she heard Salvador's excited intake of

breath. So Lucky Ruiz had not forgotten his promise. She felt strangely disturbed.

Friday of that week fell on All Souls Day, November 2. An important holiday in Mexico, it was the day when the family dead returned to their homes.

Aunt Consuelo and her family did not observe the day at all. Lupita had no photograph of Papá, so she could not even light a candle decorated with a black ribbon to honor him either. The night before the Day of the Dead Mamá would set her candle alight in front of his picture and put out a glass of water for his thirst, some food to nourish him, and incense to guide him home. She and Uncle Antonio would go to Mass the next morning with their neighbors, who would honor their own dead.

But not Lupita and Salvador! No, they must go to work, not to church. That Saturday dawn found them riding to yet another field of crookneck squash. Neither Salvador nor Lupita had anything to say to the others in the back of the truck, but Elvio laughed and joked as usual.

As they arrived at the field, Lupita whispered to Salvador, "Mamá should have my latest letter by now!"

"Sí, Lupita, she must have the money." Salvador got out of the truck and stalked off to get in line for the food boxes. His tone was angry. He had been angry since Wednesday, speaking sharply to Lupita when she tried to talk to him. Even the Ruiz children kept out of his way. Getting that cardboard box of brightly colored shirts, jackets, and trousers from Lucky had not helped his temper. The clothing fit and was of better quality than anything he had ever owned, but it was not what one wore to harvest crops. Salvador still dressed in Papá's clothing when he went to the fields, but Lupita could tell by the way he put on the black-and-white check coat and the felt hat that he disliked them for their shabbiness. *Ay de mí*, Salvador despised Papá's coat. How could he?

When Lupita returned from the fields, she found Irela waiting on the front steps, her chin resting on her fists, her elbows on her knees.

When the others had gone inside, Irela said, "Lupita, the stores are open now. If you'll buy me an ice-cream sundae, I'll help you get a dress to wear to church."

"Ice-cream sundae. What is that?" asked Lupita, who had never heard the words before.

"Something made out of ice cream, a sweet."

"What does it cost?"

"Seventy-five cents for the kind I want."

So much! Lupita shook her head in dismay. That was almost a half-hour's pay. But she must have a dress. If she got one today, she could go to Mass tomorrow.

"*Sí*, Irela," she agreed despite her misgivings. Who else would go with her to the store? Elvio? No. Catarina? No. Catarina would make fun of her, no matter what she bought. Aunt Consuelo? No! They might not be able to find a Spanish-speaking clerk.

Lupita washed her face and hands, and then she and Irela walked the mile and a half into Indio to the big *gringo* discount department store. Irela confidently led Lupita to where the women's clothing was sold. Lupita, afraid not only of *la migra* but of the *gringa* sales clerks, hung back while Irela pulled her by the hand down the racks of dresses.

With an assured air, Irela pulled out dress after dress

150

and held it up to Lupita for size. There was no rose-pink dress of Lupita's dawn daydream, but there was a yellow one with white dots. Irela pressed it to Lupita's chest, shoulders, and waist, and then held it down to her knees for length. "Sí, this one fits you." She assumed a serious expression. "Lupita, you should try it on, but the *gringa* clerk over there says you can't because you look too dirty."

A fire of humiliation spread over Lupita's face, and she asked quickly, "What does it cost, Irela?" She gasped when she heard the price. It cost even more than the blue dress in Colton.

"It is the cheapest one here," Irela warned her, "and Elvio says this is the cheapest store in town."

"Sí, I know, I know." Reaching into her jacket pocket, Lupita pulled out her pay envelope and gave it to Irela.

They bought a cotton petticoat, yellow knee socks, a yard of yellow ribbon, and a pair of black vinyl sandals in the same store. At each stop, Irela paid out more of Lupita's earnings to various clerks.

When they had everything that Irela thought Lupita needed, Irela led the way to the store's café, where she ordered a chocolate ice-cream sundae at Lupita's expense. Lupita sipped her soft drink and marveled that she had spent over thirty-five *gringo* dollars for clothing.

As they walked home with her packages, Lupita's eyes filled with tears. How proud Papá and Mamá would be to think that she had earned so much money all by herself.

Aunt Consuelo said the yellow dress was a little long, but that they shouldn't shorten it because Lupita might still grow. Salvador glanced at her in her new finery and

151

said indifferently, *"Bueno."* Clearly his mind was else-where—on his upcoming evening with Lucky Ruiz.

After supper, Salvador washed and dressed in his new clothing very early. He began to prowl the length of the living room back and forth, and by seven o'clock he had made them all nervous.

Suddenly Lucky Ruiz arrived in his red car with a roar and a screech. He slammed the car door shut, then bounced up to the house.

"Hola, I am here!" he announced loudly to everyone. "Come on, Salvador!"

Without a polite *adiós* to anyone, Salvador walked out the open door with Lucky, leaving Lupita staring after him.

Aunt Consuelo did not seem upset at the rudeness of the two youths. She chuckled and warned Lupita, "Do not wait up for your brother. I know that Lucio will stay out all night. His father and mother were very glad to have him move out so they could get some rest."

Where would Lucky take Salvador? *Madre santísima!* Would Lucky get Salvador into trouble with the police here? There was not only *la migra* to worry about; there was also the *gringo* police.

When Señor Fidencio honked his horn the next morn-ing, two persons were still missing from the Ruiz house: Uncle Hermilio, to no one's surprise, and Salvador. At first Lupita hesitated to get into the truck, but Aunt Consuelo said shortly, "I told you not to wait for him. He'll be along."

All through Mass, Lupita kept looking for Salvador. Even when she lit the candle at the altar for Papá, her thoughts strayed to him. Where was he? Where had he gone with Lucky? What had happened to him?

To her relief, Lucky's red convertible was parked beside the house when Fidencio brought them home. Lupita sped inside ahead of her cousins and aunt. Her brother and Lucky sat at the table drinking coffee.

Lupita sniffed the air; something about it was different. There was a queer smell, but what was it? She had smelled it before. Suddenly Lupita knew. There had been an old tramp who smoked marijuana all the time in Ensenada, and he had smelled like this. The scent, even stronger than the smell of the leaking gas stove, was coming from Lucky or Salvador. Trouble was here in this room!

"*Hola*," Lucky greeted the rest of the family as they came in the door. Then he pointed to Salvador. "I stayed to tell you that Sal is going to move in with me and my other friends today. I quit my job as a dishwasher to work in a garage, and last night I arranged for Sal to take over my old job in the café."

Salvador! Leaving?

Lupita stared in horror at her brother. He was looking at the floor. Mamá had said they were to be together, and now he was leaving her!

"No, no!" she cried, and burst into tears.

Salvador got up, took Lupita by the elbow, steered her into the bedroom on the right, and closed the door. Leaning against it, he said in a low, hard voice, "Lupita, listen to me. This is work I like, work that pays me better money than harvesting squash, even more money than I got in Colton. It is a good job in a café that serves Mexican food."

Lupita wailed, "But Mamá said we were always to stay together."

"Don't make so much noise! I don't want everyone to hear us. We will be in the same town, Lupita. You will be living with a Ruiz, and I will be living with a Ruiz. Think, Lupita, I'll have more money to send to Mamá. We can go back to Mexico earlier this way."

"But *la migra*, Salvador! *La migra* came to the café in Colton!"

"*La migra* has not come to this café in a long time. Mostly *pochos* work there. If it does come, every *pocho* who works there will warn me in plenty of time. Lucky says if I got away from *la migra* one time, I am lucky by nature and I can get away again."

"Salvador, please stay here with me. Stay here! You have only seen this *pocho* two times. I do not like him. Don't leave me. I am afraid." Lupita ran to Salvador and tried to wind her arms around his waist.

He pushed her away, holding her by the forearms, and hissed, "Lupita, I don't want to stay here. They don't want me here!"

"They don't want me either. Don't forget that I hit the *gringo* robber with the water bottle to help you."

"That was a long time ago and down in Mexico. Lupita, you want a better *mañana* for us, don't you? For Mamá and the others and for you and me. Don't you want that, Lupita? *Don't you?*" All at once Salvador whirled around and smashed his fist against the door. Then he turned to face her, his eyes flashing. "Don't you want that, Lupita *Mañana?*"

Frightened, Lupita sobbed, "Sí, you know that I do."

"Then hear me. This is a way to get a better life and for

me to get more money. I cannot work in these fields any-more. I will save, so when we go back to Mexico together, we will have a lot of money to take home with us. Lucky says I can take back so much money that it will make people's eyes pop. Maybe I'll have a car to drive back home in."

"But, Salvador, I don't want you to go! I want to go where you go. I need to be where you are!"

To Lupita's horror, Salvador grabbed her shoulders and shook her. "Lupita, Mamá said for you to obey me," he said softly but angrily. "You must stay here with Aunt Consuelo! I promise you when I am ready to go back to Mexico, you and I will go home together!"

He flung her onto her aunt's bed, then picked up the cardboard box with the rest of his new clothes. With a jerk, he opened the bedroom door and left. A moment later she heard him say, "*Adiós.*"

Lupita rolled over on the bed and began to sob. She wept for hours, but no one came near her except Irela, who walked to the door after a time, looked in at her, and then shut it softly.

Lupita poured out her grief and fury. At dusk, she sat up and dried her eyes on the hem of her new dress. Then she went out into the living room.

Aunt Consuelo turned and looked at her. "Let him go," she said softly. "Men are like that, Lupita. You and I go to the fields tomorrow. Come and eat now. You must make yourself strong for work. That is what your mother would want."

"*Sí,* I know that, Aunt Consuelo." As Lupita took the plate of food her aunt handed her, she told herself that Consuelo was right. She must stay strong for the sake of

Mamá and her smaller brothers and sisters and for herself too.

Lupita knew what she must do. She must make a skin for herself against a world that could be so suddenly and unexpectedly cruel. Sí! She would trust her own instincts, which she now knew to be right, and develop a shell so hard that nothing could pierce it, not even being deserted by Salvador.

Lupita glanced at the wall opposite the table where she sat eating. There, hanging from a hook, was Papá's black-and-white coat. It had not been fine enough for Salvador to take with him. She would keep the coat, keep it and cherish it. When the day came to go home to Mexico, she would take it with her.

The days after Salvador's departure passed slowly for the heavy-hearted Lupita. Though the work in the fields had grown easier for her, she still ached from it. Yet the ache in her heart, wondering when Salvador would come to visit her, was even deeper.

At last he came, on the fifteenth of the month, but she did not get her longed-for chance to speak with him privately. She sat in her aunt's crowded living room and listened to Lucky and Salvador boast about their fine jobs and their trips to other desert towns in Lucky's car. Lupita glared resentfully at the *pocho*, but he didn't seem to see her.

Impatient, she fidgeted on the living-room daybed, waiting for Salvador to summon her outside. After about twenty minutes of trivial conversation with Aunt Consuelo and Elvio, he got up, walked over to her, and dropped a twenty-dollar bill into her lap. "Send this to

156

Mamá in the next letter you write," he mumbled, and quickly joined Lucky, already at the front door. Both youths jogged out to the waiting car.

Lupita stared after him, openmouthed. *Ay de mí*, he had refused to speak to her! She vowed that he would not evade her company so easily the next time he came.

But when he did come again, Uncle Hermilio happened to be at home. As soon as Salvador and Lucky arrived, Hermilio began to talk to Lucky in English, until Lucky interrupted to say, "Speak in Spanish. I want Sal to understand what you're saying about baseball. I'm trying to teach him about United States sports."

"Ah, *sí*." Hermilio grinned. "Did you ever play baseball in Mexico?" he asked Salvador.

"*Sí*, but I played more soccer." Salvador smiled too, apparently having forgotten that Hermilio had not wanted him in his house.

Hermilio went on. "Soccer? *Sí*, the *gringos* are just now beginning to play the game."

"I know, Uncle Hermilio," Salvador softly replied as Lupita fumed. "I watch soccer on Lucky's television set."

While Elvio and Catarina argued with their mother about buying them a television set too, Lupita kept her gaze fixed on Salvador's face. She tried to catch his eye, but he carefully avoided looking at her.

Dios, how they all chattered of television and sports— things she cared nothing about. Then Uncle Hermilio asked Lucky about his car, and Lucky started talking about valves and piston rings and carburetors. Lupita wanted to stamp her foot and shriek, "Stop!"

Finally Lucky said, "So I guess the car's all right for a while. I just put sixty dollars' worth of equipment in her and spent all of last Sunday working on her." He got up and stretched his arms. "Sal's got to get back to our place and change his clothes for work. We have to go."

Salvador rose too, ready to leave. Lupita realized that he had never intended to speak to her at all. *No*, he could not do that! Lupita stood up and said firmly, "Salvador, I need to talk to you."

He glanced at her out of the corner of his eyes, but he didn't reply. Reaching into his pants pocket, he hauled out some crumpled bills and laid the money on the table. "This is for you to send to Mamá from me. *Adiós*, everybody." Salvador turned on his heel and went out the door, which Lucky was holding open.

Aware that everyone was looking at her, Lupita walked woodenly to the table and picked up the money. There was a ten-, a five-, and two one-dollar bills. Only seventeen dollars.

"How much is it?" asked Catarina curiously. "Is it twenty dollars like the last time?"

Ashamed that in spite of his good job Salvador had given her less than before, Lupita lied, "*Sí*, it is the same."

After a week of harvesting carrots in early December, Lupita came home one afternoon and found a letter from her mother. Written by their priest, it was short, but still long enough to make Lupita content.

Mamá and all the others were in good health. She had received all of the money Lupita had sent and was glad that her children were living with Consuelo and that both had work they liked. She had kept her maid's job and was saving money to repay the moneylender. She greatly missed Lupita and Salvador and prayed for their welfare.

Lupita's brothers and sisters were looking each night for the special star they called Papá's, and she hoped Lupita and Salvador would always go with God.

Not a word was written about Aunt Consuelo's letter, saying that her house was too crowded. Mamá was very kind. She would never mention it in any letters she wrote to Indio.

When Salvador again came with Lucky two days later, Lupita marched up to him and handed him the letter the moment he stepped through the door.

He read it, then returned it to her, averting his eyes. "Mamá is all right. I knew she would be. Have you told her I am living with Lucky?"

Lupita said loudly, "No, I will not write that to her, Salvador. It would worry her that you live with a stranger. If you want to tell her, you must write her yourself."

Salvador said nothing. He reached into his shirt pocket and pulled out some folded cash. "Here, this is all I can send this time."

Lupita unfolded the bills immediately—only thirteen dollars. Each time he brought less money. Why was this?

Ay de mí! She thought she knew. A girl? She asked, speaking more softly, "Have you forgotten Dorotea, Salvador?"

At last Salvador's eyes met hers. "There are other girls, *pocha* girls, prettier than Dorotea."

So it *was* a girl, someone she didn't know.

A few minutes later Salvador and Lucio said good-bye, and Elvio went outdoors with them. When he returned, he announced, "Mamá, Salvador is thinking of buying himself a motorcycle. Lucky's found a secondhand one that he can buy cheap."

159

Lupita felt like screaming. Mamá was saving to pay the moneylender, she was working in the fields to help, and Salvador was thinking of buying a motorcycle! This is what came of his living with Lucky and the other *pochos*. Salvador's thoughts were on Indio and pleasure, not on Mexico, Mamá, or his sister.

"A motorcycle?" Lupita exploded, her fists clenched with rage.

Aunt Consuelo looked up from braiding Catarina's hair. "*Sí*," she said matter-of-factly. "It is the way of men here. First a boy gets a bicycle, then he wants a motorcycle, and then an automobile. Hermilio had an automobile for a while until he had an accident. He never got the money to buy another."

An accident! Lupita felt stabbed to the heart by the word. Even if Salvador was not hurt badly enough to have to go to the hospital, an accident would surely bring the *gringo* police and after them *la migra. Ay de mí*, was there no end to her worries? The worries that Lucky Ruiz had brought into her life were with her day and night.

Perhaps if she could talk with Lucky, she might be able to make him understand how she felt about Salvador. Perhaps she could make Lucky see the dangers in Salvador's having a motorcycle. She must find some way to talk with him, but how?

One cool, damp, mid-December day, on her way home from harvesting another field of carrots, Lupita, who as usual was thinking of Salvador, felt the motion of the truck change. Usually it ran noisily but smoothly. Now, however, it was jerking and jolting and rocking back and forth. A particularly hard jar sent her over onto her neighbor. When Lupita got up, she scooted to the side of the pickup to grab hold of the metal edge and look over the side at the road ahead.

To her dismay, Señor Fidencio did not stop behind the stop sign at the corner. The truck went ten feet beyond it, then came to a quivering halt. A driver coming through the intersection swerved his sedan sharply to keep from hitting the pickup. As he sped around the truck down the country road he blew an angry blast on his horn.

Holding on to the truck's side, Lupita watched as they lurched to the next intersection. Luckily, it was empty, and Señor Fidencio did not stop at all but crawled slowly through.

"What is it? What is wrong with Fidencio? We just went through a traffic sign," cried one of the women.

A man in the truck's rear said, "It is not Fidencio's fault. Hold on to something. The brakes must be gone. He cannot stop the car."

Lupita caught her breath in fright as another of the women wailed, "What shall we do? Shall we jump out now?" She began to stand up.

"Get down. Get down," the man shouted, getting up to pull her down beside him. "Trust Fidencio. If you jump out, you will be sure to hurt yourself."

"But what can we do, *señor*?" The woman was sobbing. "Shall we pound on the window? Shall we tell him what is happening?"

"No! Fidencio knows very well what is wrong. If you must do something, pray."

"Pray, *señora*."

While women began to murmur the Hail Mary, Lupita watched the man light a cigarette. His hand shook as he raised the match to it. Holding tight to the truck's side, he leaned over, looking worriedly at the road in front.

Looking out, Lupita saw a red light ahead. Would it turn green before they reached the intersection? She said her Hail Mary too, and as she came to the end, the light changed to green and the truck went safely through.

She turned and cried out to the man, "Where are we going?"

"Fidencio will go to the garage where his grandson works. It is on this side of Indio, not far."

Lucky's garage! In spite of her terror, Lupita felt excitement. Lucky would probably be there too.

She wanted to ask how long it would take to get to the garage, but she didn't have a chance. Señor Fidencio began to sound the horn, and Lupita turned to see what was happening. She saw that other drivers stood still as the truck rolled through intersections. No one passed the slow-moving pickup, and a long line of cars formed behind the battered truck.

When Señor Fidencio reached the outskirts of Indio, he turned slowly onto a side street. In a few minutes the pickup rolled through the wide-open door of a cavernous building made of large, pink concrete blocks.

Lupita held her breath. Would they hit something in the gloom here? She could see a number of cars, some up in the air on gleaming steel poles, others over pits in the ground, and still others parked here and there. Would anyone guess that the pickup had bad brakes? Could it be stopped before it rammed into a wall?

Men came running toward them, alerted by the honking horn. A big *gringo* shouted in English to Señor Fidencio, and at once the sound of the horn ceased. The man motioned to a barrier of tires piled up against a wall.

Fidencio steered the truck in that direction until it bumped against the tires and stopped.

They were safe! Lupita let out her breath in relief as the women in the back finished their prayers.

Señor Fidencio got out of the cab and called loudly, "*Hola*, Lucio!"

At this call, the mechanics who had surounded the truck walked off into the oil-and-gasoline scented dimness, going back to their own work.

Where was Lucky?

Becoming more nervous, Lupita tried to rub the field dirt off her face with her jacket sleeve. Though she would still look like what she was, a farm worker, at least she would have a fairly clean face when she tried to talk to Lucky about Salvador.

Lucky came toward them from the rear of the garage. He did not look so elegant here in a pair of grease-stained coveralls, but he walked in the same easy saunter. After talking to his grandfather, he motioned to the left side of the garage and walked off again.

A moment later Señor Fidencio came around to the back of the pickup. Consuelo was with him, looking relieved and wiping her forehead. Fidencio said softly, "Get down. My grandson says we will be here about twenty minutes. They will have to put the truck in the air so they can work on it. All of you must get out. It will not be safe for you inside."

"Is *la migra* here?" a woman asked in a frightened whisper.

"No, it is not, *señora*. You could fall out and hurt yourself when they raise the truck. Do not concern yourself with *la migra*. Come down, *por favor*, hurry!"

Reassured, Lupita and the others left the truck and

stood together in an uneasy group. Fidencio got back into the cab and steered while mechanics pushed the pickup over to the floor-level lifts.

Lupita looked about for Lucky and saw him a distance away, lifting the hood of another truck. He was alone. She had her chance.

Leaving the group, Lupita went over and stood beside him. "How are you, Lucio?" she asked.

He drew his head out from under the upraised hood to look at her, then at once went back to examining the car's engine.

"How are you today, Lucio?" she repeated. "I am Salvador Torres' sister, Lupita. I have seen you at our aunt Consuelo's house. I know how much my brother Salvador admires you. I want to tell you that I think you are a very good singer and guitar player." Lucky merely grunted in reply.

Speaking to his back, Lupita went on in desperation, "Lucio, I know Salvador would like you and me to be friends." Why wouldn't this *pocho* speak to her? She reached out and plucked gently at the sleeve of his coverall.

In a flash Lucky was out from under the hood, glaring at her. He hissed under his breath, "Get away from me! I don't want the boss to see you pestering me. He's a *gringo*; he hates wetbacks. Get lost, *tonta!*"

Her face afire, Lupita backed hastily away. She turned around and walked back to the group of older people clustered about Consuelo.

Her aunt was looking at her as she approached. "You should not have gone over to talk with Lucky when he is on his job," she told Lupita quietly.

Biting her lip to keep from crying, Lupita said, "I was

trying to make friends with him, Aunt Consuelo. I never get to talk with him or with Salvador either. I thought Lucky might help me see Salvador more often."

"Sí, Lupita, I know, I know." Consuelo sighed. "These young ones, the *muchachos*, want everything their own way all the time. But if you want to speak with Salvador or Lucky, you must remember that you cannot go to the places where they work any more than they can come to the fields. Do you understand that? It is not so easy-going here when it comes to working."

"Sí," was Lupita's bitter, one-word reply. She looked back over her shoulder at Lucky, who was now talking and laughing with a tall, yellow-bearded *gringo*.

"Don't be so sad," Consuelo said. "Salvador will come see you again soon. Perhaps Lucky will tell Salvador that you tried to make friends with him and that will please your brother."

Lupita stared hard at her aunt. Could she really believe such a thing would happen? She herself was certain it would not.

So far as Lupita was concerned, the rest of December was a sad time, a period of beloved Mexican holidays she missed observing.

On La Noche Buena, December 24, no costumed shepherds with bells on their staffs roamed the streets. The only way Aunt Consuelo celebrated was to go to a late Mass with the oldest children, Señor Fidencio, and his wife. Lupita looked eagerly for Salvador there, but could not find him. Lucky Ruiz was not there either. She tried to tell herself that Salvador had had to work and could not come.

December 25 came and went without a visit from

Salvador or Lucky. Lupita sent her mother twenty dollars the day after Christmas, writing that half came from herself, half from Salvador. The lie would insure that Mamá had a happy holiday, Lupita thought.

There was great excitement in the Ruiz household on January 6, the Day of the Three Kings, when children received gifts as a symbol of those the Magi had brought to the Christ child. All of the cousins expected presents.

Lupita, who had spent the previous day harvesting asparagus, was enjoying her free time. She thought that perhaps Salvador would come to visit and take part in the joy of the children, so she kept looking out the windows and listening for the unmistakable sound of Lucky's car or for the *pop-pop* of a motorcycle stopping in the front yard. But she heard nothing.

To her surprise, after all the children received their presents, Aunt Consuelo reached under the living-room sofa and dragged out a large brown-paper bag.

"This is for you, Lupita," she said, smiling.

A gift for her? Lupita shook her head. She was not a child of this house; she should not receive anything.

Her aunt urged as Lupita hesitated, "Take it. You work hard. You took Irela to the cinema. I remember. It is the Day of the Three Kings, a day of joy, so I want to give you a gift, too. Catarina chose it for you. Open the package."

While the smallest Ruiz cousins ran about the living room shrieking with pleasure over their new toys, Catarina and Irela watched Lupita open the bag. Inside was a dress, red velveteen with white cotton lace around the neckline and on the edge of the short, puffed sleeves.

Speechless, Lupita felt the fabric. Under her stroking

166

fingers, it was soft as cat's fur. It must have cost Aunt Consuelo at least twenty dollars, far too much. At last Lupita found her voice. "*Gracias*, but the dress is too fine for me. Will they take it back at the store?"

Aunt Consuelo waved her hand. "Keep it, Lupita. Wear it. Look pretty in it. You will only be young and slim one time in your life." She winked. "Perhaps some nice boy will see you in that dress and want you for his *novia*."

"Oh, no, Aunt Consuelo!"

Cartarina took up the teasing. "You do not want to have a sweetheart, Lupita?"

"No, I don't want a *novio* here."

Catarina giggled. "Your brother Salvador will find a sweetheart. If he cannot find one for himself, Lucky will get one for him. That Salvador will make the girls sit up and notice him. He is handsome."

Not wanting to hear more of Salvador and a *novia*, Lupita said *gracias* to her aunt again and took the dress into the bedroom. There she carefully slipped it onto a wire hanger and hung it under Papá's black-and-white coat.

Aunt Consuelo and Catarina would be disappointed that she did not try it on at once, but she didn't have the feeling in her heart to match its vivid color. Her heart had bled itself white with so much sorrow and trouble. It beat still in her breast, but it felt numb.

After she had held the sleeve of Papá's coat to her cheek for a brief moment, Lupita went back in to the noisy living room. She sat down beside Consuelo and, unheard by any of the others, said, "*Muchas gracias*, Aunt Consuelo, for the dress. You know that I have written several times to Mamá since I first came here?"

"Certainly."

Groping for the right words, Lupita said shyly, "Not once did I write that you and Uncle Hermilio do not get along together or that you work in the fields."

"Ah, that is good of you, little one. *Gracias*." Aunt Consuelo had dignity when she chose. She sighed. "Lupita, perhaps you will not go back to Mexico at all? Many never go back, but stay here to work and live."

"*Sí*, I know." Lupita looked away to the windows, streaming with gray rain. Yesterday had been her birthday, her fourteenth birthday, but she had told no one. Next week Salvador would turn sixteen. He and she were growing up, growing older and further apart in this alien land to which they had never chosen to come. What would become of them, separated as they now were?

13

Another letter from Mamá came toward the end of the month. The news was the same—everyone was well and she was receiving the money.

On the last day of January, Lupita came home from seven hours of harvesting cabbages. About an hour later Salvador arrived, dressed in a dark-red corduroy jacket she at once saw was new. Lupita handed him Mamá's latest letter to read. She stood with her arms folded and watched.

Not meeting her gaze, he nodded and said, "*Bueno,* Mamá ought to be able to pay off the moneylender quickly. We're doing well by her, eh?"

Her voice sharp, Lupita scolded, "Salvador, she will need money to live on even after she pays the money-lender."

He shrugged and handed her a five-dollar bill. "I need to buy some things for myself. This is all I can send this time."

Lupita looked down at the bill, and then sniffed the

169

air, smelling something over the tang of chili powder Aunt Consuelo was putting into her cooking.

"Salvador, what is that smell?" Lupita demanded.

His eyes slid past hers. "It's the shaving lotion I got on my birthday."

"One of the things you need?" Lupita's voice was scornful.

Salvador blushed and then looked angry. "No, it was a present. Tammie gave it to me."

"Tammie?"

"Sí, a girl I know here."

What a queer name! "Is she a *pocha*, Salvador?" asked Lupita.

"Sí, Tammie Mendoza. Her sister is Lucky's new *novia*." Lupita sighed. Always Lucky Ruiz.

Before she could ask more, Aunt Consuelo called her and Salvador to eat some tacos she had just made.

To Lupita's astonishment, Salvador refused. "I go to work at five o'clock tonight. Lucky will come for me in a few minutes. He's just gone to the cleaners to get his jacket. I'll eat at the café."

Aunt Consuelo was not offended. She only laughed. "Does the food taste better there, Salvador?"

"No, but there is more of it."

She chuckled, then said, "*Bueno*. If you don't eat, it means more tacos for the rest of us. You come here, Lupita. You eat his tacos and yours, too. You need to put some meat on your bones. She's too skinny, isn't she, Salvador?"

"Sí, Lupita has always been skinny."

Catarina, of course, took up the teasing. "Lupita says she doesn't want a *novio* here, Salvador. She must think

170

she's so skinny that no boys will ever pay attention to her."

"I told you I don't want anyone," Lupita burst out. The taco was burning her hand.

Ignoring her, Aunt Consuelo spoke to Salvador. "Your sister never goes anywhere to meet anyone her own age. All she sees are the old men who harvest with us. Hermilio never brings anyone home—when he comes home. All of Elvio's friends are too young. Lupita has no friends her own age, not even girls like herself." Consuelo folded her arms and planted herself firmly in front of Salvador. "Look here, you are Lupita's brother. You left my house and your sister to live with Lucky Ruiz. I think you should do something to see that Lupita also has friends, as you have."

Lupita stared at her aunt in wonder and held her breath, waiting to hear what Salvador would say.

"Lupita goes to Mass, doesn't she?" he mumbled.

"How would you know? You're never there! Sí, she does, and she comes right back here with us. Lupita does not meet anyone at church."

Salvador shifted from one foot to the other. Lupita felt a glow of satisfaction at his discomfort. He had left her to work as a dishwasher and to have good times with fellows his own age. He had deserted his sister, leaving her to do the kind of work he despised. All his talk about saving money was just an excuse.

He threw open his hands and asked, "Aunt Consuelo, what do you want me to do? I haven't got a car to take Lupita anywhere."

"Have you got yourself a motorcycle yet?" Consuelo demanded.

"Not yet."

How Salvador was scowling. Lupita stifled a giggle.

"Why can't you and Lucky take Lupita somewhere in Lucky's car?"

"Lupita is too young to go around with us. We take out girls our own age. Lucky wouldn't want to take Lupita. It is his car." Salvador's face had taken on a dark, sullen look, and his eyes flicked constantly to the door.

Aunt Consuelo turned to Catarina. "Go and bring out the dress I got for Lupita for the Day of the Three Kings."

"Sí, Mamá."

Catarina hurried into the bedroom and came prancing back, holding the hanger with Papá's coat on it and the red velveteen dress underneath. Catarina jerked off the coat and dropped it to the floor. Then she twirled the wire hanger to make the dress revolve in front of Salvador.

Lupita put down her taco, ran to retrieve Papá's coat, and held it to her breast while she listened to her aunt.

"Look what a beautiful dress this is. Lupita has had it since the Day of the Three Kings, but she has never once put it on. What good does it do her on a hanger?"

"Sí, it is a fine dress," Salvador said, with no show of interest.

Aunt Consuelo nodded. "It *is* a fine dress. Fidencio told me today that there is to be a dance, a *baile*, next month on the day of Saint Valentine. Lucky will play his guitar there. Is this true?"

"Sí, there is such a dance," Salvador mumbled. "Lucky will play when the musicians stop to rest."

"And you will be going to this dance also, Salvador?"

"Sí."

"Why don't you take Lupita?" Aunt Consuelo asked, to Lupita's horror.

172

"*Lupita?* I am going to take Tammie Mendoza!"

"Have you asked this Tammie yet?"

"Not yet."

"*Bueno*, don't ask her. Let someone else take her. You can take your sister instead."

Lupita looked from face to face, her fingers trembling as they held Papá's coat.

"No, no," she cried out, "I don't want to go to the *baile*."

"Be quiet, Lupita," her aunt ordered. "Salvador, you take your sister to the *baile*. You can get Lucky to pick her up in his car. Lupita can dance with many boys you and Lucky know, and you can dance with this Tammie Mendoza. Get Lucky to take both her and her sister. There must be one of Lucky's friends who does not have a *novia* now. Perhaps Lupita would like him."

"No," cried Lupita, but no one paid any heed to her.

Salvador raised his head. "*Sí*, there is Rafael. He works in the automobile tire store next to Lucky's garage. He has no sweetheart now."

"*Bueno*, then there is somebody for Lupita to dance with! You can find many partners for her." Aunt Consuelo smiled, then lifted a warning finger. "But, Salvador, see to it that she dances only with boys that you or Lucky know."

Having won her way, she turned in triumph to Lupita. "So you are going to a *baile* in your new red dress."

"I don't know how to dance, Aunt Consuelo." That should put an end to the plan. It was the truth. She had never learned anything but a few Mexican country dances at her school, and she was sure that everyone would be dancing *gringo* style at the *baile*. So many of the young *pochos*, Lucky and Elvio and Catarina among them, seemed to her to be half-*gringo*. And now Salvador. . . .

Aunt Consuelo waved her hand. "Elvio and Catarina can teach you to dance. They know all the dances. You have two weeks to learn." Consuelo turned her head to Salvador. "I bet you know how to dance the *pocho* dances, don't you?"

Catarina hooted as she danced in a circle around Lupita, whisking the red dress about as if it were a partner. Lupita looked past her cousin at her aunt's beaming face. Aunt Consuelo had meant well, but she did not understand how Lupita felt. Who was this Rafael? Lupita asked herself. What would he be like? Another Lucky? *Ay de mí*, no!

Aunt Consuelo said, "Lupita, a girl never forgets her first *baile*. You will never forget this one, I promise you."

Salvador didn't wait to hear more. He turned on his heel and stormed out of the house.

Lupita ran after him. "What's wrong with you, Salvador? What's happening to you?" she cried.

"Nothing, nothing," he muttered, then ran forward to get into Lucky's car, which had just pulled up.

Elvio and Catarina were delighted to teach Lupita to dance. When one tired, the other took up the task, putting Lupita through her paces. As soon as their school bus dropped them off in the late afternoon, they turned on their father's radio, found a *gringo* dance-music station, and set about teaching her not only the *gringo* dances, but also *la salsa*, the fast-moving dances much favored by young California *pochos*.

Though she was often weary after her day's work, Lupita paid close attention. She enjoyed learning to

174

dance more than she had thought she would. She even learned to like the *gringo* music once she became accustomed to it.

By February 13, Elvio pronounced her ready to go to the *baile*. At least, she would not humiliate Salvador or Rafael by her poor dancing.

Lupita had written Mamá nothing of her quarrels with Salvador. She continued to send what money she could, chiefly her own earnings. By denying herself all treats, she managed to mail close to the same amount she and Salvador had previously sent together. But now she wrote that they were going to a *baile* on the day of Saint Valentine. That would please Mamá and make her think all was well between her and Salvador.

Lupita put down her pencil and took a deep breath. She would try to make her shell very hard against whatever might happen at the dance. But perhaps she need not. She might enjoy it after all.

Saturday afternoon, Saint Valentine's Day, the Ruiz household was in a bustle. After Lupita had come home from the fields, she showered, washed her hair, and got into her petticoat. Carefully she put on her first pair of nylon panty hose while Aunt Consuelo braided her hair and pinned the braids on top of her head. Then Lupita slid into the red-velveteen dress. It fit her fairly well, and the deep color made her gold-toned skin glow. Lupita looked at herself in Consuelo's small bathroom mirror and was amazed to see that she looked pretty. Though she had no coat to wear, Consuelo loaned her a black, hand-crocheted shawl for the occasion.

With Irela beside her, Lupita sat in splendor on the

old sofa while Consuelo sat across from her, admiring her handiwork. Catarina and Elvio had gone to the cinema with Fidencio and his wife, but before they left Elvio had inspected Lupita and said, "She looks okay, Mamá."

Aunt Consuelo and the younger children waited in the house with Lupita. Time went by, and still Salvador had not arrived. Finally, the youngest cousins went sleepily to bed. Lupita looked nervously at Consuelo, but her aunt only said, "He'll come."

At nine thirty Lupita heard the rattling sound of Lucky's car pulling into the yard. Then Salvador was at the door. Dressed in a dark-blue coat and trousers, pale-pink shirt, and deep-red tie, he looked like any other *pocho* she had seen at church. He gave Lupita a quick look from her crown of braids to her black sandals, grunted, and said, "Come on then."

"Have a good time," Aunt Consuelo called after them, as they went out to the car.

"I ride with Lucky in the front," Salvador said curtly. "You get in the back seat, Lupita."

"Where are the other girls?" asked Lupita, peering into the empty back seat.

"We took them to the dance first. Then we came after you," Salvador replied.

"Salvador, where is this Rafael I am to meet?" Lupita nervously grasped her brother's arm.

"At the dance with the girls. Get in. Hurry up, Lupita." He shook off her hand and got in the car.

Lupita opened the convertible's rear door and sat down. Without a glance behind him, Lucky put the car into gear and rapidly turned it around in the yard. The sudden motion threw Lupita off-balance and sent her sprawling

176

across the slippery plastic upholstery. As she got up, she was struck by a powerful rush of cold air. Instantly chilled, she pulled the shawl over her head as far as possible, then sank down out of the wind.

By the time they reached the hall, she was covered with gooseflesh. As Lucky searched for a spot in the brightly lit parking lot, Lupita sat up and let the shawl fall onto her shoulders. She strove to calm herself and to put a look of confidence on her face, but her teeth wouldn't stop chattering.

Once Lucky parked the car, he and Salvador got out. Without a look at Lupita, Lucky started swiftly toward the hall.

Salvador opened her door and said, "Get out now, Lupita. I'll take you inside to meet Rafael. He was dancing with Tammie when we left so he couldn't come along." Lupita saw a muscle at the corner of her brother's jaw tighten. Salvador did not like the idea of anyone else dancing with Tammie. "Come on. Hurry up, Lupita."

He reached into the pocket of his trousers and brought out a pale-green ticket, which he shoved into her hand. "I paid your way in to the dance. Give this ticket to the man at the front door." He turned and headed toward the noisy hall.

Lupita got out of the car slowly. She was frightened. Salvador seemed to hate her, and the hall would be full of strange *pochos*. Her stomach felt filled with ice. But she went to the door Salvador had gone through and showed her ticket to the man. He smiled down at her, and she took courage from his smile.

Suddenly she felt Salvador's hands snatching away Aunt Consuelo's shawl. He gave it to a gray-haired lady, who

177

put it on a shelf above a long row of coats on hangers. Salvador grabbed Lupita by the wrist and pulled her out of the anteroom to the very edge of the dance floor.

Lupita gasped aloud. Hundreds of people filled the room; they stood along the walls or danced under a ceiling festooned with red and white crepe paper.

Almost everyone was young, and they were dressed in their very best. The boys looked as elegant as Salvador and Lucky, and the girls wore beautiful long dresses of peach, turquoise, yellow, pink, violet, blue, green, and white. Some glittered with silver and gold sequins. The air was like a flower garden, filled with their perfumes.

Lupita became painfully aware of how she looked: her short dress, the flat-heeled shoes, the old-fashioned hairdo. She had no glittering earrings or bracelets.

"There is Rafael now, over there with Tammie!" Salvador cried. Still holding her by the wrist, he hauled her along the edge of the floor to the opposite side of the room. A short, heavy-featured *pocho* stood next to a tiny, black-haired girl, wearing a pale-blue satin gown and a rhinestone tiara in her hair.

"Rafael, this is my sister, Lupita." Salvador took Tammie's hand and pulled her onto the dance floor.

Rafael stared, unsmiling, at Lupita. Then he asked in a husky voice, "Do you want to dance?"

"*Sí.*"

He walked onto the floor, and she scrambled after him. A moment later they were dancing to *la salsa* music. Lupita, feeling grateful for her dancing lessons, smiled tentatively once or twice, but Rafael did not look her in the eye. As the orchestra went into a second *salsa* tune, Lupita noticed that Rafael gazed over her shoulders at the other couples around them. He called out twice, "*Hola*, Rosita," "*Hola*, Marina."

When the music ended, Rafael took Lupita by the elbow and steered her away from the other dancers, who were waiting for the next tune. He led her to a row of wooden chairs against a wall. There he bowed, said, "*Gracias*," and sauntered away.

Lupita looked about in panic. What was she to do now? Where was Salvador? She could not spot him or Lucky Ruiz in the throng of waiting dancers. They must be at the other end of the hall. There was no cause to be afraid, though. Salvador would soon see Rafael without her; then he would come looking to see how she fared. *Sí*, it would be best to stay exactly where she was. She might as well sit down. Except for two older women, who were deep in conversation on her left, she would be the only person seated in the long row of chairs. She would be easy to find.

But Salvador did not come. No one Lupita knew came up to her. Some *pochas* in pretty gowns walked past her and went in a door at her right. Lupita leaned over and saw a picture of a lady with a fan in her hand. Above the picture was the word *Señoritas*. *Sí*, the room was a bathroom for ladies.

Before long the orchestra started to play again. This time the music was slow and gentle, a dreamy tune. The lights of the hall dimmed, and the dancing couples who now embraced one another could scarcely be seen.

Lupita sat in her chair while *pocho* youths walked past her, peering at her briefly, then continuing on their way. She stared through them, her face flaming, hoping none of them would ask her to dance.

At last the lights came back on full strength, and the band began to play more fast *gringo* dance tunes. Lupita stood up. She could see Lucky dancing, but she could not spy her brother at all. Ah, there he was, dancing with Tammie. Her tiara glittered icelike in the overhead lights. Lupita wondered if she should get closer to Salvador, but decided she had better not. He would not like it if she did.

Suddenly Rafael danced by with a long-haired girl in a flame-red gown. He was smiling and talking to her, a different fellow from what he had been with Lupita. Watching them, Lupita felt her throat grow tight. *Sí*, Rafael had thought her skinny and ugly, and compared to the *pochas* here she was. Her dress was short, and she wore her hair in Mexican braids, not floating and loose. What did Aunt Consuelo know about what *pochas* wore to *bailes*?

Tears of misery rose in Lupita's eyes as she sensed a dark truth. Neither Salvador nor anyone else would come over to her. He and Lucky had known Rafael would not like her. Perhaps they had arranged ahead of time for her to spend the evening sitting in a chair. Salvador was not going to have his good time spoiled by his sister.

Blinded by tears, Lupita stumbled into the empty ladies' room. Its window was open and she gulped the cold air. How fresh it felt after the warmth of the hall. Lupita went to the washbasin, turned on the cold-water tap, and mopped at her eyes and cheeks with a damp paper towel.

Looking at her image in the mirror, she stared at her swollen eyes. Never again would she cry over Salvador, she vowed bitterly. She no longer had a brother.

Lupita crumpled the paper towel and threw it into the

big metal basket. She opened the door and stepped into the crowded room. A blast of music greeted her as the band started a new tune. At that very instant the music changed, faltering into discord and winding down to a slow, wailing finish. The dancers stopped, frozen for a moment into a pattern of waving arms and lifted legs.

Something was wrong. Lupita froze, her eyes widening. What was it?

All at once she heard a metallic braying sound, a shout. "*La migra. La migra!*" Words in English and Spanish thundered through a bullhorn. "We are the United States Immigration Service. Stay where you are. Do not run. *No corres.*"

La migra!

Using her back and shoulders, Lupita pushed open the door behind her and slid into the ladies' room. A moment later she hauled herself up to the windowsill and threw her leg over it. Dropping to the ground, she crouched in a thicket of oleanders planted just under the window.

La migra! It had not come to the fields or the church or to the cinema or to the café where Salvador worked. It had come to the *baile,* where there would be many people, some of them wetbacks.

Lupita bit her fist and wondered if Salvador had escaped. She waited for what seemed to be a long time before she heard automobile doors slamming and cars leaving. Was *la migra* going away or were some *pochos* leaving the dance? Could she come out now? No, better wait for a while. Lupita squatted in the bushes until she heard the orchestra start up again.

As she was about to rise, she heard voices coming toward her. Two men were speaking in Spanish. One was Lucky Ruiz. He said heavily, "Okay, Rafael, so *la migra* rounded up Salvador. That was bad luck. I liked him."

Lupita wanted to howl. Salvador had been caught. What she had feared since she had first heard of *la migra* had happened.

Lucky went on, "People in my grandfather's family are going to think that I'm responsible for that *tonta* sister of his. I couldn't find her in the hall. Where did you get rid of her? Maybe she's out here."

The two *pochos* stopped in front of the oleanders. Lupita could see their feet. Rafael said, "I took her over to the chairs and left her there. Maybe *la migra* got her, too. It's not being able to speak English that gives them away." Rafael chuckled, obviously unconcerned about Lupita's fate. "I guess I'll have to take care of Tammie Mendoza now."

An icy, shuddering rage swept over Lupita. What did these *pochos* know about the trouble she and Salvador had been through? What did they care? She rose out of the oleanders, parting them with her hands. "I am here, Lucio, Lupita Torres, the *tonta* wetback." Lucky jumped to hear the voice behind him. He turned and Lupita went on, "It's too bad Salvador had to spoil your evening by getting caught. I don't want to stay here where you and Rafael are. Just take me to Aunt Consuelo's right now."

Lucky cast a guilty glance at the other youth. "Rafael, go get Lupita's shawl. It's the black one. Tell Tammie and her sister that I'll be back later on to take them home."

"Okay, Lucky, okay." Rafael hurried off, glad to be away from Lupita's accusing eyes.

Minutes later Lupita was sitting once more in the rear seat of the red convertible, wrapped in her aunt's shawl.

Lucky put the key in the ignition; then he turned

around. "It happens all the time, Lupita, that *la migra* catches wetbacks here in town. Your brother's a smart one. He will make his way here again. You wait and see."

Lupita answered icily, "Señor Pocho, what do you know of how hard it is to get into the United States? You do not know what it is like to live in Tijuana and have no work. I am not so sure that Salvador will get back over the border again."

Lucky turned back, started the car, and drove through Indio without speaking another word. Lupita let the cold night wind blow on her and stared at the sky. In front of the Ruiz house, she opened the back door and got out. Lucky roared off.

There was a light on in the living room. Holding the shawl about her, Lupita went up to the front door and stepped inside.

Aunt Consuelo was lying on the bed in the living room, listening to the radio. Irela lay beside her with her face to the wall.

As Lupita entered, her aunt sat up and asked, "Back so soon, Lupita? Didn't you have a good time?"

"*No!*" Lupita took off the borrowed shawl and put it on the sofa. She said calmly, "*La migra* came to the *baile*. They caught Salvador."

"*Ay de mí*, Lupita!"

"But they did not catch me." Standing in the middle of the floor, Lupita told her aunt what had happened. She did not mention Rafael.

"Thanks be to God, Lupita, they did not get you, too!" Consuelo sighed. "Do not worry about Salvador. He will be turned loose in Tijuana."

"*Sí*, I know. He will try to come back, but it will be hard, very hard."

Aunt Consuelo interrupted Lupita's thoughts by saying, "You will stay here with us and work with me in the fields?"

"Sí, I will."

She would have to go on living with Aunt Consuelo. Mamá would want her to, more than ever now that she was alone. Besides, where else could she go? Lupita doubted that Salvador would go home to Ensenada and tell Mamá that he'd been caught and deported. No, he would stay in Tijuana and try again. But who knew if he would ever return to Indio? There were many *yanqui* towns he could go to. Tammie Mendoza could be replaced by another *pocha* as quickly as Dorotea Ortega had been replaced by Tammie.

Lupita shivered, thinking of what Rafael had said. Salvador and the others had been caught because they could not answer *la migra*'s questions in English. It was not their lack of cards, but their lack of English that had betrayed them.

"Aunt Consuelo," Lupita said. "Salvador was caught tonight because he didn't know any English. I must learn."

Consuelo nodded slowly. "But you cannot go to school here, Lupita."

"No, I know that, but someone here could teach me English when I come back from the fields."

Lupita kept silent, waiting for her aunt's reply. Would Consuelo realize that Lupita wanted to learn English for another reason, one equally as important? So she could get out of the fields and find work as a waitress, earn more money, leave this house, be as lone and independent as the ear of corn on the stalk until she had enough money to go home to Mexico.

After a moment, her aunt said, "*Sí*, Elvio or Catarina could teach you. They taught you how to dance. I will speak to them about it."

"*Gracias*, Aunt Consuelo." What more could she ask? She had the answer for which she had hoped. "I will need a book in Spanish and in English, Aunt Consuelo. I will pay for it if someone will buy it for me."

"I will ask Hermilio to get you a book. Now go to bed, Lupita. You look very tired."

"*Sí*, I am tired."

As Lupita turned to go into the bedroom, her aunt slapped Irela gently on the bottom. "You get up now, Irela, and go to your own bed."

"*Sí*, Mamá." Irela arose and padded into the bedroom next to Lupita's.

An hour later Lupita lay sleepless, waiting for Catarina to come home. How could she sleep? There was so much to think about. Would Elvio and Catarina be willing to help her learn English? It was hard to tell about them. Perhaps they would be more enthusiastic if she promised to pay them for their time and trouble. How difficult everything was. How hard to make a shell so she would not be hurt so much. How hard not to weep!

As the tears came stinging to her eyes, Lupita heard the door open. Was Catarina home from the cinema? No, the truck had not returned yet. Someone had crept silently into the small room.

"Lupita," said a small voice in the darkness, "let me in bed too."

It was Irela. Lupita sighed softly and flung back the blankets. What did Irela want? And what had she brought into bed with her? Hard, cold, slick things that jabbed into Lupita's side.

"Lupita, pull the blankets up over our heads."

"Are you that cold?"

"No. Pull the blankets up."

Lupita did as Irela wanted. She had probably come with some of her favorite toys to keep her company.

All at once the deep dark under the blankets vanished in a bright yellow light. Irela held her mother's flashlight and a thin, flat book. Lupita recognized it as one of Esmeralda's, the youngest Ruiz cousin.

Irela flopped over onto her stomach and shone the flashlight on the book. She opened it to the first page and pointed to a brightly colored picture of a boy, a girl, and a dog.

Pointing to the dog, Irela said, "This is a *perro*. The word for him in English is *dog*. *Por favor*, say *dog*."

"Dog," Lupita repeated.

"*Bueno*." Irela nodded and went on. "The *muchacho* is a *boy*. Say *boy*."

"Boy."

"*Bueno*. The *muchacha* is a *girl*. Her dress is *roja*. It is red."

"Girl. Red. *Gracias*, Irela."

"*Gracias*, Irela Ruiz, *Profesora*!" Irela corrected.

"*Sí*, Irela Ruiz, *Profesora*!" Lupita repeated. She caught her cousin in a hug.

Irela wriggled momentarily, then pointed to the boy in the picture and said, "Pay attention. His shirt is white."

"White," repeated Lupita happily. *Sí*, she would learn English now! Irela had appointed herself Lupita's *profesora*.

Let the other Ruiz cousins laugh at them both. That would mean nothing to her or Irela. Both of their tomorrows were sure to be better.

CONNECTIONS

In this author's note for Lupita Mañana, *Patricia Beatty shares some of the facts behind the story of Lupita and Salvador Torres. How did she blend information with imagination in* Lupita Mañana?

A Note from Patricia Beatty
Patricia Beatty

Lupita and Salvador Torres are real people whose story I have endeavored to tell here. I have never met them, but I have met and talked with their older brother, whom I shall call Victorio. He recounted their adventures to me some months after Salvador was apprehended at a dance and deported to Mexico. During the time this novel was being written, Victorio returned voluntarily to his home in Mexico. I do not know what has become of Lupita, but I suspect she is working somewhere in California at this moment. Her true name, of course, is not Lupita, nor was her brother's name Salvador.

To most American children (except for those in the most desperately deprived families), the poverty of Mexico would be unbelievable. However, it is a fact that there are multitudes of Mexicans who live constantly at the very edge of existence. They are found not only in the cities but in the countryside, where a corn crop failure can be a major disaster. The death of Lupita's father could easily create the crisis I described, a dilemma that could not be solved even by the expedient of child labor. Child labor is far from uncommon in poor Mexican families. Though Mexico has a public school system, many children receive no more than a second-grade education because they must leave school to work or because the upper-level schools are located too far from where they live. (Poor Mexicans do not own automobiles.)

To these desperately poor Mexicans, the United States represents the country of financial opportunity. They flock to the Mexican border towns, hoping to cross over to find jobs that pay high wages. A few men are given permission to cross the border as temporary agricultural workers. But the Mexican national who does not have a special card permitting him to work in the United States can remain here for no more than seventy-two hours. Consequently, those others who want to work in the United States must come over as illegal aliens.

The immigration problem is complicated in the United States. On the one hand, illegal aliens take jobs that might be filled by young Americans. On the other hand, American employers claim that only aliens will work at certain necessary jobs. They say that they cannot stay in business without such workers. State and federal authorities are currently studying ways to solve the problem, and one suggestion is amnesty for those illegal aliens who crossed over prior to 1970. As of 1980, it is unknown what the decision will be.

Thousands of Mexicans are living illegally in the United States, and each month thousands more attempt to cross the border. There are many methods of doing so. I have written of only two, those used by the real Lupita and her brother. Hiring the services of a coyote is one way, but it is very expensive for the would-be immigrant. Some

Mexicans are able to pay the coyote outright. Others pay him after they have found work in the United States. The means of enforcement of such illegal repayment for an illegal service can be imagined. It is dangerous for an immigrant to fall behind on his payments to the coyote, who reaches at times into the United States to punish the person holding out on him.

The coyotes work through a network of people on both sides of the border. Not all the exploiters on the United States side are Mexican Americans; some are non-Hispanic Americans who are in the trade for the profit.

Getting across the border with a coyote can be dangerous. The horrifying first attempt of my characters is factual. Such attacks by American bandits on wetbacks occur periodically near Chula Vista, California, in Dead Man's Valley, a real place.

Once in the United States, the illegal alien can find his existence a very uneasy one. As I point out, the alien must live and work, at least at first, among Spanish-speaking people. He is fortunate if he can come to members of his family. Many aliens do just this; relatives help them find work and provide a home and security. The formality of getting a United States Social-Security card can be handled in a number of illegal ways.

Illegal immigrants work in a variety of low-paying jobs, such as janitorial services, kitchen work, textile operations, and lawn-care services. They are generally paid less than the United States minimum wage by their Spanish-speaking employers. An alien rarely complains to the employer, since he or she is afraid of being reported to the United States

Immigration and Naturalization Service, *la migra.*

La migra operates throughout the United States, seeking illegal aliens of all nationalities. Mexican men who are caught are handcuffed and driven to the border where they are held for a time. They are easily identified not only by their lack of documents, but also by their inability to speak English. Agents commonly ask Mexican-appearing people where they were born. Women and children are not held but simply escorted back into Mexico. Entire families are deported at the same time.

It is very common for a man to cross over, find work, and then bring his family one by one, or two by two, until all are together. The children of known illegal aliens working in the United States can attend schools in some American communities, provided the parents pay tuition. In other places children are admitted free, but usually they do not go to school at all for fear of being discovered.

It may seem strange that children the ages of Lupita and Salvador come to the United States looking for work, but it happens. Homeless Mexican children inhabit the parks and the nightmarish cardboard slum that lies in the dry bed of the Tijuana River, waiting for a chance to cross the border. Their misery is increased when the riverbed floods, as has happened several times during the past few years.

La migra is a constant fear to aliens in the United States. The service conducts raids, going into places where the presence of Mexican aliens is suspected. The agents invade cafés, factories, social events—anywhere Spanish-speaking people gather. My informant, Victorio, told me that *la migra* even went into Roman Catholic churches until the protests of the clergy stopped the practice.

I have visited the towns used as locales in *Lupita Mañana:* Ensenada, Tijuana, Colton, Indio. Also I found helpful material in *Time, Newsweek, Atlantic, Harper's,* and other magazines. Issues of the *Los Angeles Times,* which included the account of the railroad yards, were particularly useful to me. Back issues of the *Los Angeles Times* and the *Riverside Press-Enterprise* contained invaluable descriptions of the living conditions of the Mexican American field workers in and around Indio.

Hermilio Ruiz is no more typical of Mexican American men of his generation than his brother Fidencio. Each is an individual portrayal. It is, however, a sad fact that many Mexican Americans become prematurely aged by the heavy manual labor they do and by their poverty, which can lead to poor nutrition. Their physical ailments are often neglected for fear of high medical bills, and they tend to rely on home remedies of dubious worth. Not surprisingly, rheumatism and arthritis are frequently found among middle-aged Mexican Americans who have done labor for years.

■ ■ ■

*The smell of simmering rice, the strumming of a guitar—
these are part of the mountain town of Jalcocotán in
western Mexico. Ernesto Galarza (1905–1984) lived in
Jalcocotán when he was a boy. Which parts of this account
remind you of* Lupita Mañana? *of your own childhood?*

A Childhood in Jalcocotán
from Barrio Boy
Ernesto Galarza

Like many other mountain pueblos, Jalcocotán had no
school. Once the village had sent a committee to Tepic to
petition the government for a teacher. The committee
assured the government that the neighbors would be
willing to build the school themselves and to provide the
teacher with a place to live. Once in a great while, when
the *Jefe Político*, who represented the government, visited
Jalco he would be asked very discreetly and courteously
about the petition. The answer was always the same: "It is
under consideration." Many years had passed—how many
no one really knew—and Jalco still had neither teacher nor
school when we went to live there.

Reading, writing, and arithmetic were held in great
esteem by the *jalcocotecanos*. A few adults in the town had
finished the third or fourth grade somewhere else. They
taught their own children the ABCs and simple arithmetic
with the abacus. For writing they had the *pizarra* and the
pizarrín—a small square of slate with a decorated wooden

frame and a slate pencil.

Books were rare. My mother had one, which she kept in the cedar box. It had a faded polychrome drawing on the cover with the title *La Cocinera Poblana*, a cookbook which had belonged to Grandmother Isabel. We did not need it for cooking the simple, never-changing meals of the family. It was the first book from which Doña Henriqueta ever read to me. The idea of making printed words sound like the things you already knew about first came through to me from her reading of the recipes. I thought it remarkable that you could find oregano in a book as well as in the herb pot back of our house. I learned to pick out words like *sal* and *frijoles*, *chile piquín* and *panocha*—things we ate. From hearing my mother repeat the title so often when she read to us, and from staring at the cover drawing, I guessed that the beautiful girl in the colorful costume was the *Cocinera Poblana*. The words above her picture were obviously her name. I memorized them and touched them. I could read.

For me and my cousins until we were six, book learning was limited to a glimpse now and then of my mother's cookbook. Our school was the corral, the main street of Jalco, the *arroyo*, and the kitchen.

We learned to roast coffee on the *comal*. In the back of the house we kept a large basket of green coffee beans covered with a straw mat. Every few days my aunt scooped a bowl of the beans and spread them on the hot griddle. We took turns stirring them with a long wooden spoon. When the beans were toasted to a shade of rich brown, which my aunt called *el punto*, she took over. Too much brown and the coffee would taste burnt. Too little and it would taste raw. While this was going on the incense of coffee filled the house.

The toasted beans were then stored in an earthen pot covered with a cloth and a lid. Every afternoon a portion of this supply was measured out and chucked into the coffee grinder with the bronze cast-iron dome, the crooked handle, and the tiny wooden drawer. We took turns at the daily grind to give us enough fresh coffee for the next three meals.

The green coffee and other staples of corn, beans, and rice were kept in rattan baskets along the back wall where it was always coolest and darkest. From a rafter there usually hung a stem of bananas, the king-sized ones called *platano grande.* Braids of red peppers hung there also, and white onions. Three boards resting on pegs made a shelf where we kept the bundles of cornhusks and the dried herbs. Stashed somewhere in the larder there was always a jar of raisins and some vanilla pods which appeared in the kitchen only on special occasions. From this storehouse came the foods and aromas of Doña Esther's kitchen.

Watching her I learned to cook rice. She poured a cup of water into the rice bowl and churned it with a spoon to rinse it. In a clay frying pan the cooking oil was already sputtering, and in it the washed rice was spread and stirred constantly until it turned a light brown. The rice was then covered with boiling water, salted, peppered, seasoned with minced onions and set on a side burner of the *pretil* to simmer. The grains of rice came out of the pan crisp and whole, the mark of proper Mexican rice.

* * *

If you were past six and going on seven, life in Jalco could be made disagreeable by neighbors who seemed to think that they could scold you and tell you how to behave. You never knew when a *compadre* or *comadre* of your aunt, or your uncle, or your father, or your mother was watching. For that matter, even people who were not *compadres* to your family thought they had some sort of rights over you. If you did or said something slightly irregular at the farthest end of the street from your cottage, where your legitimate bosses lived, somebody would be watching and ready to call out: "Mira, que muchachito tan malcriado." And if the offense was considered serious, the voice would say, "You will see, I am going to tell your mother." In a village so full of snitchers and busybodies, you could get an extra ear pull for any trivial breach of good manners—the *buene educación* which the adults prized so highly.

As a result you paid attention to what was expected of a *muchachito muy bien educado.* You never broke into an adult conversation. This was called putting your spoon in, or the way I remember the rule: "Los muchacitos bien educados no meten su cuchara." No one ever entered a house or left the room without saying "Con su permiso." It was "with your permission this" and "your permission that" practically all day long, unless you were playing with your friends. Whoever called you, for whatever reason, if you answered "what do you want?" you were in trouble. You had to answer by asking for a command: "Mande Usted?" People talked to one another on the street in low tones; only drunks and *muchachitos mal educados* raised their voices, or the *arrieros*, when they shouted to their donkeys.

Every mother in the village could ask you to do an errand. If I was in the middle of a game, or just sitting in the street watching the *zopilotes*, some neighbor would call me: "Ernesto, come here and take this to Doña Eduvijes." What right she had to order me around no one ever explained, but I was taught to move right up, answer "Sí, señora," and do the errand.

In fact, running errands was the special business of any boy or girl between the ages of four and six. When you delivered something you always began by saying, "My mother sends greetings and says may God give you a good day, and here is an egg." When you reported the accomplishment of your mission, you repeated the other half of the ceremony by heart: "She says that she sends greetings, how is the family, and many thanks for the egg." Any neighborhood courtesy—an exchange of a banana for a red pepper, or the return of a borrowed utensil—was sure to pass through our messenger system.

Some errands were special. Going for milk was one. There was one cow in the village. She was stabled in a corral on the arroyo side of the town, where she could be walked across the stream and tethered in the pasture beyond. No family drank milk every day, only when there was pudding or chocolate to make on feast days. It seemed to work out smoothly, with just enough milk whenever it was wanted, because nobody wanted much. I went to the one-cow dairy with a small pitcher about quart size. The cow was milked straight into it, nobody minding the flies or manure among the cornhusks that littered the corral. On the walk home the important thing was to avoid the pigs and dogs and hens with strict attention to getting the milk home unspilled.

We did not have an orchestra in Jalco, though even the *Huicholes* had them in their villages. But there was always music. Somebody on the street owned an ancient guitar that Doña Henriqueta said was from before the time of the Aztecs, which was several hundred years. The *jalcocotecano* who owned the guitar tried hard year after year to learn to play it. In a feeble voice he sang to the "kaplink-kaplunk" of his instrument, and everybody on the street listened, mostly out of sympathy.

In a class by himself as musician was my Uncle José. The mouth organ we bought for him from the *varillero* became, under his direction, as close as anything we ever had to a town orchestra. José never had any lessons. He heard the *arrieros* whistling on the trail, the ballads the mariachis played in San Blas and Tepic, the country poems set to music which the women sang, and the cries and calls of the birds. He imitated pig grunts, Relámpago braying, Coronel sounding his morning call, and the "kaplink-kaplunk" of his fellow artist down the street. Out of the double row of small square holes of his harmonica, José sucked and huffed the repertoire of *corridos* and lullabies and marches he carried in his head. He gave concerts for me and my cousins back of the corral or down by the arroyo, as we watched the harmonica flash back and forth cupped in his long thin fingers. José always began by working his mouth as if he was rinsing it, clearing his throat, and spitting with an explosion of his cheeks. He

tapped the harmonica, which he kept wrapped in a piece
of cloth, holding it upside down, then giving each side
of the instrument a swipe on his pants. When he played
his Adam's apple bobbed up and down, keeping time to
the music.

These recitals were special events. The music we heard
every day were the songs my Aunt Esther, my mother, and
the other women of the village sang. Singing went along
with the washing of clothes in the arroyo and the kitchen
chores. . . . In one of these songs, a cicada who lived in
a chink of a wall piped a sad tune that always ended up
with "chee-ree-bee, chee-ree-bee." There was one about a
learned crow who made pens out of his quills and earned
a comfortable living writing letters for people who had
never gone to school. Another was about a peacock who
snubbed everybody because he roosted at night in a
Cup of Fire tree all by himself, a splendid perch for a
magnificent bird. A hurricane blew the tree down, and the
peacock had to sleep on the ground "just like any other
animal," said the song—a lesson for egotists.

Doña Henriqueta sang about an ugly dwarf who hid
in the top branches of a *guamuchil* whenever six lovely
elves danced around the tree to their musical rhymes.
Their favorite was the one that went:

"Mondays and Tuesdays and Wednesdays make three;
Thursday and Fridays and Saturdays, six;
We are as happy as happy can be."

Everything depended upon keeping the rhythm perfect,
but the old imp high up in the tree would groan at the end
of the verse:

"And Sunday's seven."

This, my mother explained, was like poking your spoon into a conversation and had to be punished. The elves finally caught the mischievous dwarf one night when he was climbing the tree, and they beat him with a stick until he promised to cooperate. They made him learn a new punch line, which he sang out from the top of the *guamuchil*, so that the song now sounded like this:

The elves: "Mondays and Tuesdays and Wednesdays
               make three;
            Thursdays and Fridays and Saturdays, six:
            We are as happy as happy can be;
The dwarf: "I'm in a terrible, terrible fix."

When some of the *compadres* got drunk, usually on Sundays, there was singing in some corral or in the plaza. Women and children took no part in these affairs, which sometimes ended in fights with machetes. We couldn't help hearing the men's songs, which became louder with the drinking. They sang the *corrido* of Catalino, the bandit who stood off hundred of *rurales*, the mounted police who chased him up and down the Sierra Madre year in and year out. In his last battle, Catalino was cornered in a canyon. From behind a boulder he picked off dozens of rurales with his Winchester, taking a nip of *aguardiente* between shots, and shouting to his persecutors: "Acérquense, degraciados aquí está su padre." The rurales, like anybody else, did not like to be called wretched punks especially by an outlaw who boasted he was their father. In Mexico for such an insult you paid with your life. They closed in until Catalino lay dead. They chopped off his head and showed it in all the puebloes of the Sierra Madre, which made Catalino hero enough to have a ballad composed about him. It was generally agreed that he was from Jalcocotán where the bravest men were to be found, especially on Sunday nights when they were drunk.

■ ■ ■

For years, the first stop for many immigrants to the United States was the immigration center at Ellis Island, now a museum. Here, some of those immigrants speak for themselves. What did they hope to find in America? Do people hope to find the same things today?

Oral History Project: Ellis Island

On January 1, 1892, Annie Moore, a 15-year-old girl from County Cork, Ireland, was the first immigrant to land at Ellis Island, America's newest immigration processing center. Situated on a small island in the upper New York Bay, Ellis Island was to become the main port of entry for over 12 million immigrants who passed through its doors until its closing in 1954.

Upon landing at Ellis Island, an immigrant was examined by a doctor to check for serious health problems or contagious disease. If he or she was in good health, the immigrant would then report to a government inspector, whose job it was to determine if that person was eligible for admittance to America, based on U.S. immigration laws. Immigrants denied access to America had the right to appeal their case to the Treasury Department in Washington, D.C. If passed by the doctors and the inspector, immigrants were usually processed in about five hours and admitted to the United States. Others were detained for treatment in one of the island hospitals, held until relatives came to claim them, scheduled for legal hearings, or, in 2 percent of the cases, refused admittance.

After its closing in 1954, Ellis Island was left to the

elements and to vandals. In 1965, President Lyndon B. Johnson declared it a national monument, and in 1983, the National Parks Service began its restoration. Opened as a museum in 1990, Ellis Island is truly a tribute to the "melting pot" that is America.

The Ellis Island Oral History Project began in 1973 as an informal collection of interviews with people who had immigrated to this country through Ellis Island. The project picked up steam in the late 1980s with the restoration and preservation of Ellis Island by the National Parks Service. Over 1,200 interviews are on file; more than half of them have been conducted since 1990.

The interviews span a wide range of experiences and include the memories of people from all over the world. Many describe their first impressions of Ellis Island and of America from the perspective of the child they were then; others interviewed came to this country as adults. The interviews explore living conditions in the old country, the voyage to America, and experiences on Ellis Island, as well as early years in the United States, overcoming language barriers, and struggling to make ends meet.

Some of those interviewed were detained at Ellis Island for medical reasons; others were detained for political reasons, primarily during the 1940s and 1950s. Interviews with employees who worked on the island are also included.

The Oral History Library is a national treasure of our cultural heritage. It is an invaluable resource for students of American history, as well as for those who want a better understanding of the immigrant experience. For more information on the Ellis Island Oral History Project, write to Ellis Island Oral History Project, Ellis Island Immigration Museum, New York, New York 10004[1]

Oral Histories

"My father, who had by now moved from New York to Milwaukee, was barely making a living. He wrote back that he hoped to get a job working on the railway and soon he would have enough money for our tickets. . . . I can remember only the hustle and bustle of those last weeks in Pinsk, the farewells from the family, the embraces and the tears. Going to America then was almost like going to the moon. . . . We were all bound for places about which we knew nothing at all and for a country that was totally strange to us."

Golda Meir
Russia
Arrived in 1906 • Age 8

---

[1] Be sure to check the address before sending any correspondence.

"When I was about 10 years old I said, 'I have to go to America.' Because my uncles were here already, and it kind of got me that I want to go to America, too. . . . I was dreaming about it. I was writing to my uncles, I said I wish one day I'll be in America. I was dreaming to come to America. . . . And I was dreaming, and my dream came true. When I came here, I was in a different world. It was so peaceful. It was quiet. You were not afraid to go out in the middle of the night. . . . I'm free. I'm just like a bird. You can fly and land on any tree and you're free."

Helen Cohen
Poland
Arrived in 1920 • Age 20

"Coming to America had meaning. I was a kid of seven and in contrast to what I had gone through, Ellis Island was like not a haven, but a heaven. I don't remember any fright when I got to Ellis Island.

"My father's dream and prayer always was 'I must get my family to America.' . . . America was paradise, the streets were covered with gold. And when we arrived here, and when we landed from Ellis Island and [went] to Buffalo, it was as if God's great promise had been fulfilled that we would eventually find freedom."

Vartan Hartunian
Turkey (Armenian)
Arrived in 1922 • Age 7

"I feel like I had two lives. You plant something in the ground, it has its roots, and then you transplant it where it stays permanently. That's what happened to me. You put an end . . . and forget about your childhood; I became a man here. All of a sudden, I started life new, amongst people whose language I didn't understand. . . . [It was a] different life; everything was different . . . but I never despaired, I was optimistic.

"And this is the only country where you're not a stranger, because we are all strangers. It's only a matter of time who got here first."

Lazarus Salamon
Hungary
Arrived in 1920 • Age 16

■ ■ ■

Lupita knows the importance of family; so does Charlie Wingfield, the narrator of this oral history. Wingfield's story recalls an experience in rural Georgia in 1968. How well would Wingfield fit into Lupita's world? Read on and judge for yourself.

My Hands Are Like a History Book
Charlie H. Wingfield, Jr.

There was nine of us kids in the family and we all had to work a lot. I flunked two grades in school because of the unjust system we had to live under. I stayed out of school a lot of days because I couldn't let my mother go to the cotton field and try to support all of us. I had to decide which was more important, getting an education or letting my mother suffer alone. When my father stopped working I had to stay out of school more than ever before. I picked cotton and pecans for two cents a pound. I went to the fields six in the morning and worked until seven in the afternoon. When it came time to weigh up so to speak, my heart, body and bones would be aching, burning and trembling. I stood there and stared the white men right in their eyes while they cheated me, other members of my family, and the rest of the Negroes that were working. They had their weighing scales loaded with lead and the rod would always be pointing toward the sky. There were times when I wanted to speak but my fearful mother would always tell me to keep silent. The sun was awful hot and the days were long. It was like being baked in an oven. When I went to bed at night I could see bolls of cotton staring me right in the face.

I would look at my sisters and my heart would say . . . dear sisters, I wish you could have and enjoy some of the finer things that life has to offer. I would look at my brothers and my heart would cry . . . oh brothers, if you only knew what it's like to live and enjoy life, instead of working like bees all the time to stay alive. Then I would look at my parents and my heart would utter . . . some day I'll build you a castle and you never have to bend your backs in another field. Last and least I would think to myself. I wished I had enough money to help the poor, build a playing center and a new church for our community. All these wonderful thoughts made me forget about my sorrow troubles but as I stop day dreaming I would be the saddest guy in the whole world.

My hands are like a history book. They tell a countless number of sad sad stories. Like a flowing river they seem to have no end. The cost of survival was high. Why I paid it I will never know.

■ ■ ■

Hot sun, heavy loads, sore muscles—Lupita comes to know well the life of a field worker. At an even younger age, Rose Del Castillo Guilbault went to work in the fields. Here, she describes her experience. Are the rewards of that labor worth the strain?

Field Work
Rose Del Castillo Guilbault

El fiel' was what my parents and their friends called it— their Anglicism for the field. The first jobs I ever had were working el fiel'. I grew up in the Salinas Valley, where if you're young and Mexican, the only available summer jobs are agricultural work.

Although there is absolutely nothing romantic about working the fields, it did offer a fertile environment for learning important life lessons about work, family values, and what it means to grow up Mexican in the United States. The fields were the stage where life's truths were played out—the struggles, hardships, humiliations; the humor, friendships, and compassions. For many young Mexicans, field work is practically a rite of passage.

I can remember with uncanny clarity the first time I worked in the fields. It was the summer of my eleventh year, and I was feeling despondent and bored. I wanted to go on vacation, as many of my classmates did, but my parents couldn't afford it.

My mother was sympathetic; she was yearning to see her family in Mexico. She came up with the idea that we could earn the $50 we needed for Greyhound bus tickets to Mexicali if we both worked the garlic harvest that was about to begin on the farm where we lived.

The first hurdle to earning the money was persuading my traditional Mexican father to let us do it. He had made it clear to my mother that he did not want her to work. To him, a working wife implied his inability to support his family.

To this day, I have no idea how she convinced him that it was all right. Maybe it was because the job was very short-term—five days—or maybe it was because we hadn't been to Mexico in more than a year. My father knew an annual visit to see relatives was my mother's lifeline. In any case, my father agreed to lobby his boss the next day to let us join the garlic-picking crew.

The boss was skeptical about employing us. Not because he was concerned about hiring a woman and a child; he worried more about our inexperience and stamina. After all, this was a man's job and he had a deadline. What if we slowed things down and he had to keep a worker for an extra day?

"Since when is picking garlic such an art?" my mother retorted when my father told her that night about the boss's reservations. But then he added that the boss had decided to take a chance on us.

We started immediately—at 6 A.M. the next day. The August morning was cold and gray, still shrouded in damp fog. We wore layers of clothes—a T-shirt, a sweat shirt, a windbreaker—to protect us from the early-morning chill and later discard when the afternoon sun got too hot. We wrapped scarves around our heads and topped them with knit caps. This was our field work uniform, and it is the same uniform you'll see men and women wearing today as you drive by California's valley fields.

A foreman showed us the proper way to pick garlic. "You hook your sack to this special belt. This frees your hands so you can pick the garlic and toss it into your sack."

We watched carefully as he hooked the bag to his waist and sauntered down the row, stooping slightly, while his hands whirled like a harvester machine, making garlic bulbs fly from the ground into the sack.

"Easy!" he said, straightening his back.

And I learned it was easy—until the sack started getting full. Then it not only wouldn't stay on the belt hook, it became nearly impossible for a skinny eleven-year-old to budge.

I spent the morning engineering ways to keep the bag around my waist. I tried belting it and looping it on different parts of my body with my scarf. But it was hopeless; at a certain level of fullness, the thing just couldn't be moved. So I resorted to a more laborious yet effective method. I'd drag the sack with both my hands, then run back and forth, picking handfuls of garlic and depositing them in the stationary bag. I must have looked as silly as a Keystone Kop.

I heard laughter echoing from the distant fields. I looked around, wondering what the joke was about, and slowly realized they were laughing at me! My stomach did a somersault when I heard the impatient crunch of the foreman's boots behind me. Was I going to be told to go home?

"No, no, you don't do it right." He gestured wildly in

front of me.

"But I can't do it the same way you do. The sack's too heavy," I explained.

Suddenly men's voices called out: "Déjala, hombre! Leave her alone, man. Let the kid do it her way."

The foreman shrugged, rolled his eyes upward, and walked away, muttering under his breath. My mother walked toward me, smiling. It was lunch time.

After lunch, the afternoon sun slowed me down. Perspiration trickled down my back, making me itchy and sticky. It was discouraging to see everyone passing me, working row after row. Afternoon dragged on as heavy as the half-filled garlic sack I lugged.

By the end of the day, my shoulders felt as if someone had stuck a hot iron between them.

The following days became a blur of aching muscles and garlic bulbs. The rows seemed to stretch like rubber bands, expanding with each passing day. My mother's smile and words of encouragement—a salve the first few days—no longer soothed me.

Even at home I felt overpowered by the insidious garlic. It permeated my skin and clothes. No matter how much I scrubbed, the garlic seemed to ooze from my pores, the odor suffocating me in my sleep.

On what was to be the last morning, I simply couldn't get out of bed. My body was so sore that the slightest move sent waves of pain through my muscles. My legs were wobbly from all the bending, and my shoulders felt as if they had been cleaved apart. My whole body was one throbbing ache. The field had defeated me.

"I just can't do it," I sobbed to my mother, the tears tasting like garlic.

"Anything worth having is worth working for," she said gently.

"I don't care about the vacation. I'm too tired. It's not worth it," I cried.

"There are only a few rows left. Are you sure you can't finish?" my mother persisted.

But to me the few rows might as well have been hundreds. I felt bad about giving up after working so hard, but it just didn't seem fair to pay such a high price to go on vacation. After all, my friends didn't have to.

My mother was very quiet all day. I'd forgotten it was to have been her vacation, too. My father was surprised to see us sitting neatly dressed when he came home. He listened quietly to my mother's explanation, and after a thoughtful pause said, "Well, if we all pitch in, we can still finish up the rows tonight, right on schedule."

As I looked at my father's dust-rimmed, bloodshot eyes, his dusty hair and mud-stained overalls, I was overwhelmed with a strange mixture of pity and gratitude. I knew by the slope of his shoulders he was very tired from his own grueling field work. And finishing up our leftover work was nothing short of an act of love.

I was torn. The thought of doing battle with the field again filled me with dread. But I said nothing, swallowing my reluctance until it formed a lump in my throat.

That summer evening, the three of us worked side by side, teasing, talking, laughing, as we completed the task. It was dark, and we had grown silent by the time the last of the garlic sacks were lined up. The rosy glow from the setting sun made me feel as warm as the relief of knowing the work was finally over and done.

I worked every summer thereafter, some in the fields (never again picking garlic!) and later in the vegetable-packing sheds, always alongside my mother. Working together created an unusual bond between us. And through this relationship, and relationships with other Mexican families thrust into this agricultural society, I got an education as solid and rich as the earth we worked.

■ ■ ■

As you read about the West Side community in this poem, picture it in your mind. Why does the speaker love it so much?

West Side
Naomi Shihab Nye

In certain neighborhoods
the air is paved with names.
Domingo, Monico, Francisco,
shining rivulets of sound.
Names opening wet circles
inside the mouth,
sprinkling bright vowels
across the deserts of
Bill, Bob, John.

The names are worn
on silver linked chains.
Maria lives in Pablo Alley,
Esperanza rides the Santiago bus!
They click together like charms.

O save us from the boarded-up windows,

this pistol crack in the dark backyard,

save us from the leaky roof,

the rattled textbook which never smiles.

Let the names be verses

in a city that sings!

■ ■ ■

Patricia Beatty

■ (1922–1991) ■

Patricia Robbins Beatty was born in Portland, Oregon, on August 22, 1922. Because her father was a Coast Guard officer, the family moved often during Patricia's childhood. On several occasions, they were stationed on American Indian reservations. Beatty's days on the Quileute reservation, in fact, inspired her first book, *The Indian Canoe Maker.*

Beatty attended Reed College, where she studied literature and history. She taught both of these subjects and later worked as a reference librarian. In 1950, she married John Louis Beatty, a history student at the University of Washington. The two had actually been born in the same hospital, seven months apart!

Marriage and motherhood took Patricia Robbins Beatty away from her beloved library. When she turned to writing, she decided to write for young people. Much to her surprise, her first book sold! When her second story was also accepted, Beatty became a full-time writer. She went on to write more than fifty novels.

Beatty wrote about the history that she loved so much. She thought that historical novels were a wonderful way to help people learn about the past, and she worked hard to make her novels as accurate and as entertaining as possible. Always the teacher, she sometimes included additional comments, giving her readers more details about each novel's historical background, sources that she used in her writing, and explanations of details that she changed to fit the needs of her plot. (You can read the note that she wrote to the readers of *Lupita Mañana* in the Connections section of this book.)

Most of Beatty's novels are set in the western United States in the nineteenth century—an exciting period of national growth, frontier exploration, civil war, and industrial development. *Lupita Mañana*, published in 1981, however, was different. When Beatty's editors suggested the topic, Beatty did firsthand research instead of library research. She interviewed many Mexican immigrants, gathering their stories for use in her novel.

Beatty and her husband worked together on several novels set in eighteenth- and nineteenth-century England, which was his specialty. Their collaboration began when she asked for his help with research on a story set in London in 1752 and grew into a full coauthor relationship.

The central figures in Beatty's novels are always young people, often between the ages of ten and sixteen. Beatty's long experience with students taught her that they like to read about characters their own age or just a little older. Most of her characters are strong and independent. War or other outside troubles often separate her young heroes and heroines from their parents, forcing the children to be self-reliant and to grow up quickly.

Beatty won a number of awards for her work, including a 1974 award for her lifetime contribution of lasting value to children's literature from the Southern California Council on Literature for Children and Young People. Her novels *Jonathan Down Under*, *Charley Skedaddle*, and *Campion Towers* won individual awards.

Patricia Robbins Beatty died in 1991.